TRISH MCCARTY

Praise for

THE STARSHINE EFFECT

"Can you imagine a different world where people respect and are curious about one another, rather than afraid? I have never seen students purposely get up out of their seats to greet someone across a room, like they did for me; a result of *'The StarShine Effect.'* With a little more training these kids could become world-class leaders." **Stephanie Hendrie** President, The Hendrie Method for Exceptional Speaking

"In 2003, I had five felonies on my record and was on my way at age seventeen to an adult federal penitentiary at a cost to taxpayers of about $70,000 a year. I became President of the StarShine Mustard Seed Garden and learned to do things to help others. I now have no criminal record and I am raising my two-year-old son. My long-standing goal is to be a part of the FBI. I had no idea how intelligent I was before I attended StarShine and actually learned about how important I am." **Former student** of StarShine

"StarShine embodies the lifelong work demonstrating ethics, of my wonderful grandfather, Barry Goldwater. I am proud to be involved in this movement."
CC GOLDWATER (Producer) Sweet Pea Films. Her first film, MR. CONSERVATIVE: GOLDWATER ON GOLDWATER, is a documentary that offers an intriguing glimpse into the public and private life of Senator Barry Goldwater. Ms. Goldwater has served as a television entertainment correspondent in New York for "Live! with Regis and Kathie Lee," and in Los Angeles, Hollywood.

"STARSHINE ACADEMY is such a bright place in my own mind because it is a constant reminder of education as a means to a life that all of our forefathers always thought possible...the pursuit of happiness...it is the natural order of things." **Vernon Parker**, Former Asst. Secretary, USDA, Civil Rights, Former Mayor Paradise Valley

"I think the most important thing that STARSHINE demonstrates to our international students, is that we could duplicate this outstanding demonstration of specific methods that support a philosophy of creativity and peace building, over and over again, so that world peace and happiness would surely be the outcome." **Kellie Kreiser**, Director, Thunderbird Global Management School with Afghani Business Women visit with Thunderbird and STARSHINE

"StarShine Academy is the prototype for education done right. Children who are educated through the StarShine program will be successful in life. StarShine Academy leaders have kept their eyes on the prize, which is youth who are ready to succeed in life, who have learned the skills and who have the dream. I wholeheartedly support the StarShine Academy as a model demonstration of systems to be duplicated." **Mark Anderson**, After serving eight years in the Arizona House of Representatives, Mark Anderson was elected to the state Senate where he served as chairman of the Family Services Committee and as chairman of the K-12 Education Committee and as a member of the Appropriations and Human Services Committees, in the House of Representatives. He is currently serves in the Judicial Branch as a Justice of Peace, in Arizona

"I have written and lectured about my book, _Creative Communities_ all of my life along with my mentor, Frank Lloyd Wright. Trish and her team have created the prototype each of us can follow. This book, _The StarShine Effect_ made me laugh, made me cry and helped me to grasp the very magical essence of what a miracle teacher StarShine really has been for all of us." **Vernon Swaback**, Architect, Author, Lecturer, Former CEO Frank Lloyd Wright Foundation

"I offered to edit this book because I was curious about what was in it. I had heard about StarShine and how it was changing people and I wanted to know more. I called Trish a few days later and told her it was one of the most important, powerful books I have ever read." **Cinda Firestone**, Author, Playwright, Humanitarian _Cinda attended Sarah Lawrence College where she was a member of the Strike Committee that closed down the school in protest against the Vietnam War. She also was jailed during the Columbia University anti-Vietnam War uprising, and devoted her senior year as editor of the college newspaper to getting rid of the new President of Sarah Lawrence - who was an ex-Vice President of IBM who believed that artists could be replaced by machines. Shortly thereafter, the events of_

Attica began and Cinda decided to make her own film documenting the prison take-over. She was just 23 years-old at the time.

"I have spent my life as an educator, as a teacher, principal, coach and superintendent and as the current Assistant Commissioner of Education for Colorado. I had to spearhead many of the issues created by the results of the Columbine High School shootings in 1999 and have spoken throughout the world about prevention of children involved in crime. A key factor in childhood crime is lack of self-discipline combined with lack of self-worth. One of the boys involved in the shootings, Klebold, wrote in his journal, "I have always been hated, by everyone and everything." I am a Leadership Trainer for the Dale Carnegie Center of Excellence. When Trish called me to tell me she wanted to open a school to use as a demonstration of the most cutting edge ideas to not only educate our children academically but help them to realize their importance to society and to be a part of a global change in K-12 education, I thought she was crazy. But I have known Trish for a long time as the sister of my wife, Darlene, and I have watched her accomplish impossible things. I told her that I would risk my career and my accomplishments to stand beside her and to assist her on her board of directors, because I think StarShine is one of the most important ideals ever tried in education." The Late, **Dr. Gary Sibigtroth,** Assistant Commissioner to the Colorado Commissioner of Education, Leadership Trainer, Dale Carnegie Center of Excellence, former StarShine Academy Board of Directors.

"I have been researching and speaking for excellence in K-12 education for over forty years as co-founder of Marzano Research Laboratory, hoping to make a profound and lasting effect in improving K-12 education and teaching. Although I have sold many books and workshops, very few schools have implemented our research school-wide as StarShine has. I only wish other schools would more readily share best practices and researched results for the benefit of all teachers and students." **Dr. Robert Marzano,** Co-Founder Marzano Research Laboratory, author, lecturer, researcher

Trish A. McCarty

THE STARSHINE EFFECT

Teaching Happiness As Success

ALSO BY TRISH MCCARTY

Strategic Partners in the E Commerce

Totally Rich

Just Plane Yoga

StarShine Field School Teacher Training Manual

For Diane & Robert —
Thank you so much for
your incredible gifts
you have given to all
of us —
Love, Trish
McCarty

TRISH A. MCCARTY

THE
STARSHINE
EFFECT

Teaching Happiness As Success

Paige M. Gutenborg Harvard

Published by Paige M. Gutenborg Harvard Book Store Press
Cambridge, Massachusetts
www.harvard.com
and StarShine Press www.StarShinePress.com

www.TheStarShineEffect.com
Copyright © 2012 Trish McCarty

Printed in the United States of America on acid-free paper

Cover Design by Scott Lerman, www.LucidBrands.com

First edition, 2012

ISBN: 0-9826133-34

ISBN-13: 978-0-9826133-37
Library of Congress Control Number: 2012941513

DEDICATION

To My Parents: Ruby and Amos Doyle Sanders;
Every child should be so blessed.

For My Children:
Gene, JohnDylan, Dory and Courtney;
Every mother should be so blessed.

For My Husband:
Steve McCarty
For Making My Heart Sing

And

To all StarShine sowers everywhere; realizing dreams through education and growing tomorrow's superstars. "Then you will know the truth and the truth shall set you free." John 8:32, The Holy Bible

CONTENTS

Acknowledgments   i

PART ONE:

1 THE AWAKENING   9

2 WHAT WE NEED IS LOVE SWEET LOVE   31

3 SLEEPING WITH AN EDUCATOR   43

4 TECHNOLOGY   65

5 KISS: WHAT DIFFERENCE DOES STARSHINE MAKE   73

7 THE WOW FACTOR: WHAT MAKES STARSHINE DIFFERENT?   79

7 AN UNINTENTIONAL LEAP OF FAITH   85

8 MEETING WITH THE PRINCIPAL   89

9 DESIGNING BEAUTY AND CREATIVE COMMUNITIES   99

10 CHAORDIC DESIGN AND THE FIBONACCI SERIES   107

11 BRANDING STARSHINE   119

12 PARTNERING WITH A ROCK STAR   127

13 STARSHINE GOES GLOBAL   135

14 AFRICA WILL CHANGE THE UNITED STATES   141

15 BACK TO THE USA   151

PART TWO:

16 VALUES NOT RULES: STARSHINE FIFTEEN GUIDING PRINCIPALS   155

APPENDIX   262

ABOUT THE AUTHOR   265

ACKNOWLEDGMENTS

My parents always said, "Make friends with people who don't look or act like you, it will make your life a whole lot more interesting." We, at StarShine Academy Schools have made history. We have cracked the code of what must be taught as early as possible in order for our lives to work, and we have done it within and in spite of a very tight budget and the archaic rules for standardization in K-12 education. And we have done it by putting together every age, nearly every race, many customs, many theories and many experts sharing one desire: "We must teach our children and our adults, how to produce balanced, self-reliant, happy, intelligent, independent thinking, internally motivated, curious and wonderful, human beings."

Here, I barely mention, as there is so much more to say about many, many, more; a few of the wonderful and refreshingly weird people who have helped me to shape this destiny and this book.

First, above all, thank you to my crazy, fantastic, rockstar husband, **Steve McCarty**, who continually changes words and writes poems to make me laugh and sing and never, almost, complains about the time I spend on my computer or at work. He has helped me immensely.

Thank you **Very Reverend Rebecca McClain** for making me do StarShine. You are truly a wonderful friend and one of the too few of the cloth that constantly spreads the real teachings of **Jesus**, especially the one about loving one another and especially the children.

Thank you **Robert and Kim Kiyosaki** who gave me cash and bet me on a dare to try to change K-12 education. Check them out at _www.richdad.com_ and _www.richwoman.com_ They have helped so many people live beyond their wildest dreams, including me.

Thank you to **Michel Sarda** for making me meet him every week to gently push me to work on this book and to get it done.

Thank you, thank you my dear **Cinda Firestone**, so talented a writer, for being my editor and helping me so much to finish this book. _www.cindafirestonefox.com_ And thank you for teaching StarShine Kids Theater.

Thank you **Susan French, Heather Devich, Joyce Buekers** and the **Harp Foundation** for your friendship, your constant prayer and hands-on help. Thank you **Joy Bancroft, Cheryl McArthur,** and

Merilyn Chilleen, Ann Bitters McElhinney, Mareen Mulvaney, Esther Slater Browning, Shari Christie, April Lowry Kilfoyle, Liz Draeger, and StarShine Sharon Bacher for our MasterMind Group your love, your friendship, your prayers and your constant cheerleading me.

Thank you, especially to **Dr. Byron Davies,** for helping me to research everything all of the time and for traveling with me to Stanford, Sante Fe and who knows where else. You are a brother to me. **Jack Ring,** you truly are one of the five smartest people on earth and what a blessing you have been to mentor and guide me into better understanding the ways of nature; the ways of God working in and through us. **Vernon Swaback,** thank you for agreeing to take this ride with me and for never, ever giving up on me, in spite of the scariness of moments. It has seemed for me that I have been paired with a modern day **Buckminster Fuller** in you. **Dr. James Goodman,** thank you for seeing in me a part of you. Your brilliance coupled with your passion to make a life full of making differences has given me the courage to keep walking so many times I wanted to give up. **Kedrick Ellison,** thank you for serving on my board with such a gentle strength and bringing with it a love for children, music and economic development through educating our children. **Shep Gordon,** thank you for making me laugh out loud at the L.A. Music Awards and for making me realize other change leaders have had it a whole lot tougher than me. **Darlene Sibigtroth,** my sweet sister and board member; you have supported me since I was so little, offering always to help me. Thank you for giving our family and StarShine's board, your husband, **Dr. Gary Sibigtroth.** Gary spent his life devoted to changing K-12 education and trying to help me. He was a gentleman and a giant throughout his fight with ALS. Forever, I will be grateful for you both. **Sherry Lund,** thank you for serving on StarShine's board. You are a fighter for so many causes and I am so honored to have you as a friend. **Vernon Parker,** you have risked much, many times, serving on StarShine's board and yet you have always championed on. I will never forget you flying home from Washington, DC as you served our country as the Assistant Secretary of Civil Rights, just to speak at our first high school graduation of four students. **Chuck Trautman,** thank you for being my coach and CEO MasterMind Group leader. Your fierce love of America so reminds me of my father. **Mia Martori,** thank you for being my sweet friend and StarShine's and the Institute of EcoTourism board member and my best MasterMind, most constant, prayer partner. **Dave Cornelius,** thank you for all of your help in showing me how fantastic education and multimedia can be. **Bob Fishman,** thank you for insisting that our kids go to a real radio studio for their radio show and thank you for being my constant friend and the connector of Phoenix people. **Perry Demone,** you have been a saint with the kids and the KIDSTAR Radio Network. You are continuing your father's great work in entertainment. **Maria Murillo,** thank you for being my first StarShine Angel and longest employee. **Lynne Ericksson,** I know we are related somewhere. You have more energy than any four people I have ever known. I could fill this book full of thank yous for all you have helped me with. **Dory Rockcastle,** my beautiful daughter and assistant, you have no idea how much of StarShine has developed from your teaching. Thank you for trying so hard to be so valuable to StarShine, in spite of everything you have had to overcome. **Dr. Marilyn Prosch,** how can someone so beautiful be so brilliant? I thank you for being with me for so long, for being an integral part of StarShine's board and helping me to see education through your eyes. And thank you for all of your financial expertise and especially for your constant friendship. **Dr. Leonora Farrah Ketyer,** you are truly one of the most endearing people on the planet. It has continually amazed me that you have been able to maintain your vision of what you think kids need in K-12, even after having spent so many years deep inside of the system. How did you ever keep your spirit so high for so long? You show your deep, abiding faith in all you do. You have constantly pushed me and believed in me, far beyond my own belief. You never slow down. Thank you, thank you, thank you, for serving on StarShine's board and for helping me to do the hard work that this continues to take.

Thank you, **Gita and Rachael Romero** and for my beautiful daughter, **Courtney Neugart** who planted the beginning seeds and the inspiration for **StarShine's** work and mine. And thank you, **Claire and Mia Fontaine** for writing *Comeback* as an inspiration all families need.

Thank you to my son, **Eugene Rockcastle,** for allowing me to practice parenting on you at such a young age. I so wished then as I do now, that we would have had parenting classes in school. Everybody takes puppy training when we buy puppies, but for some reason, we practice no knowledge of parenting on our poor human earthlings. You have grown into a wonderful man, husband and father, in spite of my misguidances.

Thank you to my entire amazing family, starting with **Mom**. As **Mom** reminds ALL of us every day, we are a very, very blessed family, with tons of beautiful, smart kids.

And thank you to everyone on the **StarShine Team** which includes my friends, way past the thousands now, whether for one day or for every day, you have changed the world forever because of your effort and dedication to a crazy dream we all have; to teach our children the best we have, every time, with every child. ***"Teach Your Children Well,"*** our future depends on it.

Crying Out Loud

I'm hopelessly searching
Are you my special one
I'm tired of feeling empty
Missing out on the fun

I wish you were with me
You're as bright as the stars
But I keep on searching
You're not at any bar

Home with tears on my pillow
Sitting alone in the dark
I must be a loser
Must be labeled and marked

Now I'm crying out loud
What the hell is my purpose
Can anyone hear me
Do I even make a sound

Are you still out there
Do I even exist
I look across the room at you
You turn away like you're pissed

Awake to another lonely day
Still nothing has changed
Death seems an easier way
When you're a loser.

About this poem:
very dark...very personal, a poem about loneliness today, stuck up society, being single today..is a nightmare...i know. Described and Written by Nlimbo © 2010

As I was finishing this book, it was nearly midnight and I decided I wanted to include a poem from a desperate teenager; some poem that might put into a beautiful format, discouragement felt by too many young and old people in our world today. I first looked at poems I had collected from StarShine students. I decided to look on Google as I typed in desperate teenager. I found this poem and was able to find the person who wrote it to obtain permission to use it, as it screamed out to be included here.

1

THE AWAKENING

Creativity is oxygen for our souls. Cutting off our creativity makes us savage. We react like we are being choked. There is a real rage that surfaces when we are interfered with on a level that involves picking lint off of us and fixing us up. When well-meaning parents and friends push marriage or nine-to-five or anything on us that doesn't evolve in a way that allows for our art to continue, we will react as if we are fighting for our lives—we are.
--Julia Cameron, *the Artist's Way*

It was 1998, and the height of greed, presidential lying and buying "stuff." We were watching *The Big Lebowski* and *There's Something About Mary* at the movies. "Make a difference," was a phrase nobody said; it really didn't even occur to most people to do it. And those who truly were living to make a difference were doing it mostly alone, without much fanfare or support. It wasn't the "In" thing to do at the time. Hardly anyone remembered the popular book, *The Alchemist* by Paulo Coelho from 1988, still one of my favorite about following your real dream with the core motto of the book; *"When you want something, all the universe conspires in helping you to achieve it."*

I was concentrating on my banking career and it was on a fast track, as many careers were at the time. My company had just been named one of the top performing companies in *INC Magazine* and I was interviewed for a feature article called "The Bullet Proof Business Plan" which was picked up for the front cover and distributed internationally for the in-house magazine for UPS customers. My phone wouldn't stop ringing.

Personally though, it had been a very tough year for me. My youngest daughter, Courtney, had been miserable in her school in Phoenix. She had just turned thirteen. She was very sweet and very normal at home. But every time she came home from school, she was crying about whatever happened that day. It seemed like no matter what we did to help her to cope with school and the other kids, she was exposed to another trauma. Several of the kids were getting into drugs, alcohol, partying and sex and talking to Courtney about all of it. Although she maintained good grades, she continually felt like she was inadequate. She didn't think her teachers really cared about teaching. She said she felt like a number at school, not a person. She was involved in sports, worked hard at it and did well, but continually felt, not good enough. Friends seemed to hang out at our house, but she said they bullied her at school. She did not think she was learning anything.

I found it ironic that I paid high taxes to our government to provide my own children a great public education and yet I would have to find a different, probably private, school for Courtney where she might thrive, because I knew if I left her at her school she wouldn't. I searched every late night on the Internet trying to find a fitting school for her, no matter where it was. She was brilliant and artistic and I felt, extremely vulnerable and naive. I did not want a school to kill her spirit; I wanted one that would help her beautiful spirit to flourish. No matter where I searched, the United States seemed not to have a school that matched my daughter's needs. Finally after weeks of exhaustive, frustrating research and phone calls, and several tears, I found an American school in the Czech Republic that seemed to be wonderful. It was near a lake, surrounded by huge meadows of flowers and studied music and art in Vienna, Austria, as the school was so close to the border. The Czech Republic, known for one of the top places to develop engineers was then on the cutting edge of technology, math and science in their schools. And they seemed to love and grow great kids. As much as it scared me to have her live so far from my protective mothering, I had to remind myself that my responsibility as a mother was to do the very best of my ability for my child, no matter how hard.

Although difficult, I could financially afford to pay for choices in education for my children. And I, like most parents, rich or poor, felt it was my number one priority to give my children the very best of education. I consoled myself about sending her so far away by thinking about living in Japan when I was young. I knew Courtney would benefit as I had, in learning to adapt to cultural changes and opportunities by experiencing living in a foreign country.

I did not feel that she would receive the education and safety that she needed if I kept her in schools in the United States. It angered me to feel forced to experience the agony of our separation and to have to spend so much money in order for my daughter to get a proper education, while still paying taxes to support an education system that wasted money without getting results. I thought about the mothers and fathers who couldn't afford choices for their children's education or didn't know how to find choices, and I became even angrier with the fact that our society, including me, had allowed this mess in education to happen; we couldn't even guarantee safety, let alone good academics for our own children in the United States, even when they go to school!

We stopped respecting and supporting great teachers and teaching a long time ago. We quit giving schools the support and tools they needed to grow the "American Dream" and instead allowed the *American nightmare* to become normal. I silently prayed, over and over again for someone to rescue the system before it was too late to save our country. "Who will offer to help fix this," I often wondered, worried. The answer could not have been any more unlikely.

According to my journal, it was May 10, 1998, 3:33 a.m. I awoke as I did many times, aching to talk to my father whom had been gone from this earth for over twenty years, and whom I still missed and thought about every day. I was also sad and missing my daughter, Courtney, now so far away from me in the Czech Republic and so young. All of a sudden, seemingly out of nowhere, I immediately had a blinding thought that I needed to create a company named StarShine and it had to do with something about "Making A Difference." I had such a strong desire, that I jumped out of bed and walked quickly toward my computer in the other room to register the name and to obtain a web address. I couldn't get the name StarShine.org or .com and I didn't want it to be StarShine Ltd. or StarShine Corporation so I decided on StarShineUnlimited.

The next day, I called my brother, Dale and mentioned my idea about starting a company to make a difference. He teased me about it being a weak concept for a business enterprise and I had to agree, but the idea compelled me anyway. A company built to "make a difference" seemed an unlikely concept, but maybe I would come up with something.

A while later, I called my friend, Sharon Bacher who told me that she thought the idea had some possibilities. A true friend, she suggested that we design some jewelry related to Starfish and that it might inspire some people to "Make A Difference." Larry Golsh, Sharon's husband and a famous Native American jewelry designer, artist and photographer offered to create a dedicated design for us. We sold a few to our "all girlfriends" Mastermind Prayer Group and hoped to inspire others to "Make A Difference."

I have tried to remember what might have triggered the original seed of thought of how the "StarShine Effect" seemed to have begun or what else might have influenced my dream and awakening that night. Some of "The StarShine Effect" may have started with a boy named Michael.

Michael was a six-foot, blond, blue-eyed, sixteen-year-old beautiful kid from Houston, Texas. His grandparents had sent him to an all wilderness private boarding school in Montana partly because the boy had tried to purposely kill himself by using three times the amount of heroin that would kill a typical man and he hadn't died. His grandparents were trying to save him by putting him in this expensive experiential school.

I had decided to take a few days away from by banking work and travel to this mountain school in Montana to volunteer to help some of the kids go through a student empowerment seminar during the weekend, as a process for the school. As I sat pensively with a bunch of other volunteers waiting for our names to be called and matched with a teenager, I had noticed Michael across the room as his eyes looked directly into mine with an almost pathetic, "I don't care about anything," look. Just at about the same time, they called my name and matched me with Michael. I remember thinking, "How odd, out of an entire room of over one hundred kids, I would notice and then get matched with Michael."

Experiencing synchronicity is an everyday occurrence for me and nearly everyone else associated with StarShine now but at the time seemed uncommon. We now practically consider it normal. In fact when things aren't flowing with synchronicity we notice it and try to correct it. We even tell jokes about it. Amazing events and sometimes-minor miracles are just what we refer to now as "It's StarShine." They happen most of the time. In 1993, author James Redfield wrote a book called *The Celestine Prophecy*. It became a wildly popular book about a man on a journey that encounters many synchronicities and teaches that "There are no accidents." It might even explain why you are reading this book today. But at the time, that one with Michael was so unusually powerful that I vividly recall it as if it happened yesterday and will most certainly always remember it.

Michael was tough and mean. He said and acted like he didn't care about anything. All Friday evening, I felt like we were an impossible match for each other, and at times I wished that I had not offered to go to Montana to do this volunteer work. I didn't think there was any way to get him to work on any of the exercises that they had given to us to accomplish. He was rude and obnoxious. I couldn't help but wonder why I had volunteered to do this.

The next morning was more of the same. Michael was still doing the very least that he could, but he didn't seem to be as obstinate. Maybe he had become a bit softer during the night. He obviously knew I was trying my best to believe in him.

They told us to talk softly no matter how challenging, they said to be steady. They said to tell the kids stories about our own fears, without scaring them more. They said to gently touch their hands or back, if it seemed ok, just to make human touch, contact. They told us to try our best to stay in front of their hearts, however we could maneuver it. "Just try to keep connecting," they said.

I kept going through the processes given to us, and little by little, I could see slight changes in Michael's behavior. They told us to keep our voice steady, in an almost whisper, to maintain some eye contact and to try to occasionally to touch the kids' hands, arms or backs. They said to keep the kids talking and to try to maintain a connection in our conversations. We were instructed to catch them being good or strong and to genuinely tell them things like, "Michael, it seems like you have put a lot of thought into that." Or "Michael, I can tell this is something you really care about." Basically the exercise was all about building trust and a relationship with the kids.

By late afternoon of the second day, I was exhausted, but Michael seemed like he was starting to work with me a little more. During one of the exercises, while I was talking quietly to him, Michael suddenly turned toward me, reached out and grabbed my shoulders, buried his face next to my neck, and started to sob like a baby. It shook me, I felt so incredibly sad and helpless. The depth of emotion that I began to experience was sudden and so hard to overcome; just to be able to hold myself together. Noticing that I might need some assistance, another volunteer came over to comfort Michel, giving me a chance to excuse myself. I quickly, quietly, headed for the door that lead to the beautiful, freeing, forest outside, feeling as if I might burst out crying and become a center of attention. I just wanted to get away. As I closed the door behind me, I headed toward a tree several feet from the building, hid in back of it, and I burst into tears.

I knew that Michael had just reached some sort of break-through and that because of this school and its processes, he would probably begin to heal. He had learned how to save himself. Now quite possibly he could begin to turn toward finding a life path that would work for him.

Suddenly, out of nowhere it seemed, a kind woman touched my back and told me that everything would be okay. I looked at her and said, "No it won't. Michael might be okay, his grandparents paid a bunch of money for him to attend this school and work with people who are trained to know how to help him to heal and save himself. But what about the rest of the kids out there? What about the parents who love their kids but can't afford this place? What about the grandparents who don't know about this place? What about the kids who don't have anyone to care for them at all and don't know how to get help? What about them? Who is going to help those kids save themselves?" She looked at me with bewildered eyes and she said, "Don't you know the story of the starfish?" Although, I have since learned that this is a very common story, I had never heard it, so I mumbled, "No."

She began, "One early morning a man was walking along the beach and came upon a small girl who was trying to throw several starfish back into the water. Thousands of starfish had been stranded, as they had washed up on the sand during a storm the previous evening. The man stopped to talk to the young girl and said, 'Little girl, what are you trying to do? There are thousands of starfish out here and the sun is getting hot. You know, you are not even going to make a difference.' The little girl turned toward the man as she threw another starfish into the water and she said, 'Well, I made a difference to that one.'"

"So you see, Trish, you have made a difference to Michael, and with that you can be grateful. Just think about making a difference to one person," she said. "I don't like that story" I said. "Maybe it was fine one hundred years ago, but today we have mobile phones and front-end loaders that could push all of the starfish back into the water right away and we would be able to save ALL of the starfish. There are children, too many children, and adults struggling for no reason other than they don't know what to do, or how to find solutions to help save themselves. They don't know the people who can find and pay for the information. This is crazy. If there is a way to save some kids, why can't we use the same information to save ALL kids? Why do we use mediocre information and help for kids in bad neighborhoods or who can't afford it, and great information and help for those who can? What about parents who don't know any better but end up ruining their kids' lives due to poor parenting skills? Don't you see that as long as any child is unable to access and learn to use the information that they need to grow into a great human being, that it causes ALL of us to suffer?"

Something came over me in this small speech I gave to this woman in this forest behind this tree. It was as if I was possessed. My reactions surprised her and me. It was almost as if something had snapped inside of me. Maybe in that moment, was the beginning of the *StarShine Effect*. I am sure that our experiences in our lives each and all add up to any point in time. But something huge occurred in that moment for me. It was not something I was seeking, nor wanting; it found me.

How Bad Things Are

I became increasingly and deeply interested in K-12 education and trying to find out why it wasn't working. Inquisitive by nature, I was nearly obsessed with understanding everything I could about what was wrong and right about K-12 learning. Spending hours in the library reading and hours on the computer researching everything I could find, started being normal for me. I talked to my friends endlessly about it and asked everyone I could, including on the Internet, to give me an opinion about it. I talked to any kids who would talk to me. I wrote to famous people and education writers. What caused kids to drop out of school? Who were those kids? What caused kids to skip class? Who were the kids who went on to become successful? What were they like? Why did kids take drugs? What made kids want to have sex or babies? Why did some kids get into trouble and others to do well in similar circumstances? What caused success? What is success? What could you learn in kindergarten that would affect you when you are forty years old? Believe it or not, several people told me the greatest influence in their lives was their kindergarten teacher. I would learn later, that this indeed was true even for Frank Lloyd Wright. I didn't know if that was a good thing or if nothing much happened to inspire people after that.

We are all driven to learn things that might possibly help us to better understand our own lives, and I knew this probably had something to do with the intensity to which I searched for answers. It was more than just a healthy curiosity, and daily my searching became of greater importance to me.

I, like so many others, had gone through some pretty big traumas while I was growing up. My older brother, eight years older than me, was killed in an unusual explosion shortly after he entered the U.S. Air Force when I was in the sixth grade. I was very close to him, as he was the good-looking, older teenaged, brother always watching out for his little sisters and taking me for rides with his friends in his car. I remember being numb for a long time. I had never seen my father cry before then, but for what seemed a long time afterward, my mother and father cried often.

About a year or so later, my dad had his first heart attack and although he survived, the fear we all lived with after that seemed to never go away. He had ten more. He looked and acted healthy after he survived each one. But never knowing if our family was about to be fatherless took a heavy toll on my mother and I think the rest of us. I remember constantly worrying about him and my mother and praying that he would be all right.

I think most people would describe me as one of the popular girls but I did not feel at all like I fit in. I worked hard in school at Durango High School, so I got good grades, but I never felt that smart. My high school counselor said I scored the highest in my college entrance exams in abstract and mechanical reasoning. He further explained that it was too bad, because it would have been better had I been a boy, as there weren't too many girls' jobs that required abstract and mechanical reasoning. Although I had girlfriends, I did not feel like they were true friends. I dated guys but never was crazy about any of them. I used to wonder, "If people think I am popular and I feel like I don't fit in anywhere, what must the "unpopular" kids feel like? Weird, I know, but I actually used to have those thoughts.

Then to my and everyone else's horror, I became a pregnant teenager. It was difficult for me, like other teenagers. I felt like I had disappointed my family and my friends and for a while, thought I would never be able to gain the opportunities I had once dreamt of. I prayed and was terrified that it would totally kill-off my dad.

My parents had programmed me for success. So even then, I knew that I would never drop out of school. I was not going to become a "dropout" parent. I went to the school board on my own behalf and argued for them to allow me to finish high school, in school, as it was then against the school policy to allow a pregnant girl to stay in school in Durango, Colorado. I remember being embarrassed to admit to the board that I was pregnant but bold enough to tell them that I had eleven years of schooling and I was not about to be considered a dropout. I remember thinking that if you dropout of school, no one cares if you have six years or ten years of school, you are just considered "a dropout." And I did not want a GED, because most people I talked to wished they had received a diploma instead of a GED. The board unanimously voted to allow me to stay in school. And my parents and family helped me as much as they could. Everyone highly valued education, so I had a lot of support to be able to continue to college.

I remember meeting other girls who were pregnant at the time. Many of them came from poor families who did not care so much about education. And most of them dropped out of school. Some of those girls had two or three children by the time they were twenty-one years old and I used to think about how hard they were making it for themselves and their children, as it was hard enough for me. It would be nearly impossible for any of them to ever have jobs that would give them any sort of freedom of choices. That was not going to be me, though…but where did that attitude come from? And could the other girls have had different lives if different parents had raised them? Could their parents have been raised to appreciate a good education? These thoughts always quietly haunted me.

I couldn't stop thinking about how to fix education for everyone. Trying to learn all that I could, driven by an intense desire to figure out why education had become so irrelevant and when and why, I kept searching. I began hosting my own "Education Think Tanks." I tried to bring together the most diverse people I could think of, just to discuss K-12 education and I wrote down what I learned. I met with politicians, university professors, teachers and business leaders. I wanted to find out if there was a way to "fix" our education system to something more relevant and useful. As a banker back then, I continually wanted to find out what in education wasted our money and our taxes; what didn't work. I interviewed over four hundred teachers and principals.

What I learned really truly scared me; our K-12 education "system" was and is now worse, on the brink of complete disaster and collapse, taking all of our children and teachers with it. Our country, because of the mess in K-12 education, was not going to be able to withstand the impact of so many problems and if something was not done swiftly and completely, our United States of America, as we know it, will cease to exist, due to poorly educated citizens. More government mandated tests are escalating the problem, putting the wrong kind of pressure on schools and teachers, because good test scores don't produce prepared citizens. Schools choosing to put a total focus on high or the "Right" test scores will miss the job of educating our kids for our own future; and believe me, most schools are being forced into this. As I write, I ask myself "How have we allowed this?"

Many people in the United States do not have a clue as to how fast an entire political system can fall; or any knowledge of those fallen systems. Too often, the powers that be get used to things being broken and begin to ignore not so subtle clues. Then as problems worsen, they don't know what to do. Most U.S. citizens do not have passports, so do not travel outside of the U.S. and are nearly completely unaware of world history or news and how fast it can change, and indeed has.

I am not an expert on world affairs, but having been raised by a military family outside of the United States has given me a unique perspective and strong opinion about how large systems work or don't. My parents were well read and frequently discussed our country's problems and politics, so I grew up with the idea that we all have a responsibility to stay as informed as possible about how the world inter-relates and how fast countries can change. I was raised to become involved in changing something I had an opinion about, not merely to become a complainer.

Our education system has completely lost its way. It has almost nothing to do with helping kids or our country to become successful and it has lost its ability to give any parents the right knowledge so that they know they are doing the right thing. Teachers, the most important part of the education system, are almost completely giving up, quitting their profession, as the "system" has stopped to recognize or support their gifts, passion and importance to our society. The statistics are staggering.

Currently about one-half of our kids drop out of school. Many of these kids begin to leave as early as in fifth grade. In some cities, the number of dropouts exceeds 70%. The way the statistics are reported to the general public skew these numbers so they won't look as bad, many times reporting a small segment of the population rather than all of it. Few people want to take responsibility for how poorly we are helping our children, or not. With higher dropout rates come higher crime rates and higher teen pregnancies; making more babies who continue the cycle. Because our country has ignored this problem far too long, we now have an epidemic on our hands.

"It makes no sense for China to have better rail systems than us, and Singapore having better airports than us. And we just learned that China now has the fastest supercomputer on Earth---that used to be us." President Barack Obama, November 3, 2010

Try to visit a school in your own community. Most schools won't allow you in. Of those few who allow the public to wander through the classrooms, here is a glimpse of what you will notice: kids and teachers look miserable; hardly anyone is paying attention in class. You will see kids jumping on top of other kids, bullying them or pushing them. You will notice kids sitting in the back of the classroom trying not to get noticed. You will see teachers who look like worn-out hippies, dressing without a care about the students looking up to them, shuffling their feet as if they have been depressed for years because many of them have. The system beats down teachers and kids. You might be able to introduce yourself to the principal. These people usually look exhausted but they dress a little better. Overwhelmed with paperwork and abusive kids and parents, and having spent the majority of their careers trying to prove that they are worthy of becoming a "Principal" they are now almost too tired and beaten down to do it. The passion that drove these incredible educators to take on the extra work required, knowing that they would never make much money or have the respect allotted for other professionals pushes them far beyond what they can really tolerate. Other countries consider school principals to be more prestigious than doctors or business executives, but not in "America, the Land of the Great."

I made a decision to help these students, teachers and principals and decided to get more involved in K-12 education, so I started volunteering wherever I could. I formed a company to help my education consultant friends called "Education Resources, LLC" and was hired to work part-time on a strategic task force with Arizona Governor Jane Hull and Arizona Secretary of Education, Lisa Graham Keegan. They were working on a technology program to bring computers into classrooms throughout the state of Arizona, but it was struggling and was in the news daily for something going wrong with it. They were trying to find solutions to the problems going on, so they brought me in. The program, approved by the legislature, was called "Students' First" which I thought was a great name and a needed concept.

One day, I attended a meeting to discuss the Students' First project and was trying to understand what all was going wrong with it while sitting at a table in the Governor's office with about thirty-five other people. Everyone seemed to be arguing about so many details of the project, we weren't making any progress. Agitated and wanting to get a discussion started in some sort of positive direction, I asked the group to focus on one thing, "Let's talk about who the customer is in K-12 education. Maybe if we start there we can agree on where this project started to go into the wrong direction," I said. I thought we all could at least, agree that K-12 dollars spent, should be to educate children, making them the obvious customer. This moment was one of what I call "light bulb" moments for me in this quest to help K-12 education. Not one person at that table said the customer in K-12 is the child. I could hardly believe it, but it gave me a glaring view of why our system had become such a nightmare. We had too many servants serving too many masters while the students' needs, being too young to get noticed, had been glazed over.

The dignitaries sitting at that table were an interesting mix. Many were highly recognized educators, some were "whose-who" in business and others were "education-involved" politicians. It totally astounded me that they thought education dollars' customers were taxpayers, superintendents, unions, school boards, teachers, parents, education vendors, the governor, the superintendent and other groups. But nobody, nobody, mentioned the students! I shook my head to myself, and I spoke up, "It is the kids!" I gave an explanation quickly, because I could see that I was about to cause a riot with these genuine, bright people. "Education dollars are spent, and in essence, the kids spend the dollars to become educated. The kids think that if they go to school and learn, they will have a good, productive life." I could tell I wasn't winning any friends here and this small decision is still one that drives me everyday. If people don't understand who the customer is, how can they deliver the product? And here is the true curve: the teacher is the product. That is what makes fixing "it" so complex.

Teachers need the most help; we need to help them to become the best "product" for our children to "buy." They are drowning in a sea of confusion, bad policy, bad politics and incredible bureaucracy. Keeping the teachers a wreck, keeps the kids a mess and allows for a "raping and pillaging" of the dollars in the "system." In other words, I truly believe that those having the most to gain by making the most money off of a disjointed, non-working education system make specific effort to keep it in a mess. It is layers upon layers of conspiracy and it is a scam. And we are losing our kids.

As a member of the task force, I began to visit classrooms throughout the state to talk to and learn from a number of superintendents, principals, teachers and students. It was a huge eye-opener that I did not expect. As I traveled on my days-off in banking, I became increasingly alarmed at what I was witnessing.

The schools were all very different in the way they were run. I rarely saw any shared best practices, as you see in business competitors. I don't think I saw two schools even using the same student management systems. And at that time, in 1999, very few schools used technology for anything, certainly not for the kids' learning.

The Students' First legislation was to introduce computers to every Arizona classroom and provide funding for wiring schools and purchasing equipment. But, it was a one hundred fifty million dollar-plus mess with everyone fighting about every dollar. They had not planned for any type of a bulk purchasing for one thing, so all of the schools were purchasing their own computers, wasting time, research, money and purchasing power along with training and installation nightmares. And many of the schools simply did not want technology. Every teacher, every principal and every school seemed to fight for their own way of doing things, even when it made more sense to work together to come up with better solutions for everyone.

Businesses, especially banking, had been using computers for many years, and yet schools and school districts were fighting to be left alone. I couldn't believe it. I asked one well-known superintendent at the time from one of the largest, most influential school districts, why she was against putting computers into her school classrooms. "No one has proven that computers help kids to learn," she said. "You might want to read some magazines," I said. But it made me sad. Educators were out of the loop of what works and it was getting exponentially worse, faster.

I continued to work on the five-year project until it was over, and although it may have cracked a little opening in the state's schools' use of technology for kids by becoming one of the first states to lead a technology integration movement in K-12 education, it was a disaster of misspending and political fighting. And even today, most schools use technology in small labs, not as a general tool for the kids. To me, computers and mobile phones should be used no differently than a pencil or pen…just a normal tool for learning. And just like pencils and pens, kids should be taught how to use technology in the proper way, not one that endangers them.

What I personally gained from working on this project was immense fear about my own children's future and that fueled my desire to become some sort of catalyst for changing K-12 education. Our team for the governor was on the cutting-edge of exposure to anything advancing technological ideas for education, as every vendor hoped to become a part of the statewide initiative. I was privileged to be introduced to their solutions in one way or another. Talking with the vendors gave me valuable information about why a larger solution to our education system had not occurred. They explained that it was hard to make a profit in education because it is so disjointed with each school and district being very independent of any others. In order to sell enough products into the K-12 market, a vendor would have to employ too many salespeople, making it nearly impossible to ever profit from any innovation. Most schools highly value their independency of other schools and do not share valuable discoveries or new ways of doing things. This "We are better than you are" attitude of competition among schools is deeply embedded in the system, so each vendor would have to have enough sales people to support each independent school, almost an impossible situation. There are groups who thrive on this chaos in our school systems. Keeping schools competing rather than sharing good results or practices ultimately damages our teachers, our children, our economy and our country.

According to the Education Stormfront Blog, Crudbasher explains some of my own feelings on his blogpost on Februay 25, 2011…But there is more to this story and it begins about one hundred years ago, as the Industrial Revolution was heating up. Prior to that time, the vast majority of people in the US were involved in farming. There wasn't a big need for factory workers. When the assembly line was invented by Henry Ford to manufacture cars, production was vastly improved and many more factory workers were needed. The key to the assembly line was standardization. Parts were made to exacting standards, allowing them to be interchanged. Before that, most products were handmade and each was slightly different.

In order to work on an assembly line, you had to know three major things:

    1. You had to be able to read.

    2. You had to be able to write.

    3. You had to be able to do simple arithmetic.

It hasn't changed; reading, writing and arithmetic. You needed fewer people who could manage small groups so "managers" were born. Managers needed to be better trained and they had to be good decision makers. Factory line workers were not supposed to make decisions because it would cause variations into the line. Standardization was the key above all else. But where would you get these workers in sufficient numbers? The cost to train them would be prohibitive, not to mention would take too long. Therefore a group of industrialists such as Henry Ford, John Rockefeller and most notably Andrew Carnegie began to exert their influence on education. They used their power to help shape the public education system we have today.

You can see their influence today in thousands of classrooms across the country. Children sit in neat rows and are taught the three Rs above all else. In fact while there are other liberal arts taught, they have never had the same standing as so called STEM (Science, Technology, Engineering, and Mathematics) courses; today more popular than ever. Students are grouped by age rather than skills and everyone receives a standardized curriculum. Every year they are given a battery of standardized tests (mostly owned by one very large, very politically influential testing and textbook company) and upon demonstrating a sufficient skill level (and some not) move on to the next year. Even the class day is divided into periods, which are dismissed by a bell, just like on an assembly line. These classes allow the student to get a certain amount of "credit hours" which are the basic unit of measure for education. These are called Carnegie Units and were created by Andrew Carnegie's Foundation. After the public school had finished teaching, the most promising students went to college to learn skills for management.

Is this all a bad thing? No. Mass public education resulted in the 20th century, which had the most rapid improvement in the standard of living in human history. American industry was able to achieve amazing feats of production, which peaked in World War II. During the war in one year, 1944, American factories produced over 100,000 aircraft. They produced a fleet of ships, including one that was built from start to finish in just 14 days. 25 years later we went to the moon.

But what happened next? The principles that originated in the U.S. were spread around the world. Developing countries began to make their own factories and it became cheaper to make products there and ship them to America. Manufacturing in the U.S. began to decline because labor costs were too expensive. Fortunately there was another revolution on the horizon, which promised a repeat of the successes of the industrial revolution: This is the now ongoing "Knowledge Revolution."

Once again the leaders of the "new" revolution are petitioning the powers that lead our country to provide them with workers. This time however, an existing school system is already in place. Think of the public school system as a machine. It was designed and built to produce factory workers, not necessarily successful, inspired, human beings. That's why education reform is such a controversial issue. If the public school system is designed to produce factory workers, then it's doing quite well. We have all the factory workers we need. When was the last time you heard of a factory that was hurting for workers? The problem is of course, the jobs (and our country) of this new century will require a much different type of skill set. Of course, you still need to read, write and do simple math, but in addition you need to be able to think and behave. Critical thinking was never an objective for the current school system and it isn't in other countries, either. Even though according to Jeff Dyer's *The innovator's DNA*, "Innovation is the lifeblood of our global economy and a strategic priority for virtually every CEO around the world. In fact, a recent IBM poll of fifteen hundred CEOs identified creativity, as the number-one 'leadership competency' of the future. The power of innovative ideas to revolutionize industries and generate wealth is evident from history." In China if your scores aren't high enough, you get kicked out of school, ensuring China of low-level workers in the fields, they hope. India recently created a similar law. Kind of sounds like what is happening in the United States.

According to the Broad Foundation for Education: We have low expectations for American students and you can find more on Google:

- American students rank 25th in math and 21st in science compared to other industrialized nations.
- America's top math students rank 25th out of 30 countries when compared with top students elsewhere in the world
- By the end of 8th grade, U.S. students are two years behind in math being studied by peers in other countries. This fact is pretty bad, but when you couple that with the fact that using math makes your brain smarter by doing it; it is a scary fact. My dad used to say "Math and music makes you learn how to think." He was right.
- 60% of 8th graders can't read at their grade level and most will never catch up. From what I have seen, this is getting worse.
- More than 1.2 million students drop out of school every year. That is more than 600 students every school day and one every 26 seconds.

- The poverty rate for families headed by dropouts is more than twice that of families headed by high school graduates.
- Dropouts from the class of 2007 will cost our nation more than $300 billion in lost wages, lost taxes and lost productivity.
- Each cohort of dropouts costs the U.S. $192 billion in lost income and taxes.
- Sixty five percent of U.S. convicts are dropouts and lack of education is one of the strongest predictors of criminal activity. And instead of teaching them inside of prisons; they sit and wait and do tatoos.
- A dropout is more than eight times as likely to be in jail or prison as a high school graduate and nearly 20 times as likely as a college graduate.
- For each additional year of schooling, the odds that a student will someday commit a crime like murder or assault are reduced by almost one-third.
- Each year, the U.S. spends an average of $9,644 per student ($5000 in Arizona) compared to $22,600 per prison inmate ($70,000 in Arizona).
- Increasing the high school completion rate by just one percent for all men ages 20 to 60 would save the U.S. up to $1.4 billion per year in reduced costs from crime.
- 44% of dropouts under the age of 24 are jobless.
- Over 6 million twenty-something year olds still live with their parents supporting them.
- Educators, typically are not taught how the brain learns or how best to manage classrooms; they are taught subject matter.
- It is a rare educator having the time or money to devote to success and self-motivational seminars. They can't teach what they don't know.

- Educators are entertainers, good or bad, like it or not. But most of them aren't good at it because they don't know how; they haven't been taught.

2

WHAT WE NEED IS LOVE SWEET LOVE

Don't ask what the world needs. Ask what makes you come alive and go do it. Because what the world needs is more people who have come alive.
– Howard Thurman

"It's the StarShine Effect," we tell you when you get tears in your eyes as you visit our schools or when you listen to one of the teachers describe what happens there, or even as you begin the trainings for teachers and parents there, and you start to cry. The feeling that swells up inside of you and causes you to feel an overpowering emotion seems to tap into a deep undisturbed feeling of love or love lost; a primal feeling that catches people by surprise. It seems to have something to do with their own love or dreams of possibilities, the love or hope that they forgot they needed.

What if you weren't educated? It is a hard thing to imagine or think about. And yet we all have missed out to some degree. We are not taught how to be human beings, or how to form relationships with someone or how to love to learn or listen or why we each are so important in the world right now. We are not taught how to love and appreciate others and ourselves. These things are the most important to know, but they depend on excellent parents or advisors to get them. And unfortunately, excellent parenting usually comes from being taught by excellent parents.

It is not a surprise that we have at least three generations of nearly non-existent parenting; kids trying to figure things out for themselves. And it is no wonder the world is in the shape that it is in. Broken people with limited and broken knowledge have been ruling the world. Too many people, companies and countries believe success is about accumulating stuff. Many are realizing too late they missed the very thing that they needed to know and understand, how to love and be loved. Schools didn't think to teach it because they did not know it either.

We have all known "untouchables," those people who are truly unlovable, dirty, smelly, angry, mean, no eye contact or fierce eye contact. The sad fact: the more a person has not had or experienced love, the more "untouchable" they become, creating a viscously worsening cycle. Some well-known therapies use hugging as a means to heal people. They hug a patient from ten to one hundred times a day until they see a "softening" of the person seeking the help. It seems common sense, the more love you have been given, the more you have to give. But the reverse is also true, the more love you give, the more love you get.

When a child is raised with a hug and a good-night kiss every single night, no matter whether or not they deserve it, the parent sends them several messages such as, the child is lovable no matter what, the child can depend on the parent, the child has security and the child is worthy of significance. This message carries into adulthood and into their future relationships with others, including their spouse. It is a relatively simple behavior to start at any time of your life if you want to feel more loved. Always hug and say good night.

On the other hand, if a child has been abandoned, adopted or has lost a parent for any reason, they have experienced severe trauma. Their brain will adapt by causing them to regularly exhibit flight or fight behavior, anger and outbursts. This anti-social behavior must be met with a "Time In" from a calm, steady adult, not a "Time Out." That means, simply to spend time *closer* to the child, teen or even adult, not further away. This is easier to explain than to actually *do*.

When people are angry, especially young children, they believe there is something wrong with them and are reacting against it. The worst message you can give to them is to abandon them. They need quiet, steady calmness, occasional eye to eye contact and almost any type of connecting, like cooking, cleaning something, going for a walk, working on a project and an occasional human touch. They don't need "alone time" and they will get worse if you, too, lose your temper and start telling them how undeserving they are.

Babies, when crying for food or attention, quickly get worse as we have experienced, when left unattended without attention for any length of time. The quicker their needs are met, the softer their personalities develop because they feel secure. This love attention does not "spoil" children. Learning manipulative behavior from adults who are inconsistent with their love, attention, punishments and rewards spoils children. But parents and children can change when they learn how. New, more wholesome behaviors can begin at any time, and the more they are practiced, the more normal they become.

Dale Carnegie wrote *"How to Win Friends and Influence People"* in 1936. The book was an almost instant success and adopted by many of the most powerful business leaders. It swept the nation at that time and as a result thousands of people have been trained by the organization that was built due to that book and its philosophy. If I were to tell you that the two most important predictors of any kind of success are 1)self discipline and 2)getting along with others, you would probably rationalize that taking a Dale Carnegie class might be the most important thing that you could do in order to become a success at anything. This training could have been integrated into all of K-12 education when it was first produced. Can you imagine what our country would be like today if every person that had been in grade school since the late 1930s had been able to learn from Dale Carnegie?

It should have been taught or at least something similar been required by every education institution, but it wasn't and still isn't. It would seem almost primary that we should learn to be able to get along with others or to learn how to influence one another in a productive, positive way, but we don't. Can you imagine if every grade school child had been taught this? It might have totally eliminated bullying in our schools by now. Can you imagine how our U.S. marriage statistics might have been different than they are today? Can you imagine how it might have had an effect on ethics in business and thus, our economy? It makes me wonder why such an important basis for human existence has not been made available in our schools. It makes me wonder what else is important to learn and that someone else knows but I don't.

After the experience with Michael, and continually missing Courtney, at about the same time that author Jim Collins wrote his book, *Good to Great*, and said that we have good schools, just not great ones, I became very contemplative thinking about, praying about and wanting to know if a "Great School" was even possible.

So I began to think about what would happen if I invited the very best people I could find in the world to come together to participate in several "Think and do tanks" and in their wildest dreams, create the best school possible that could reach around the world. That's when I began to organize some meetings.

The people I called on to participate in my various think-tanks were typically leaders in their own lives, many having accomplished the top accolades of their particular fields. I sought experts in every field that I could consider that might possibly have some knowledge that could be intertwined with others to produce an idea for a system design of how learn to live.

As we began to formulate a reasonable process for our meetings we started with a few assumptions. We understood and agreed that students needed to learn certain subjects in order to be able to transfer to other schools and to be ready to attend college, but we believed that the process of *how to teach* those things could be greatly improved. We also felt that if the process improved, it would take less time for the students to learn, so they would have time to learn other things, like life skills.

We began to see that the ideals previously left up to and taught by families and institutions of religious faith were all but now absent, like simply learning how to be human and social, and were now seriously needed in our schools. We needed to re-teach and re-ignite "The American Dream." But how were we going to add so much more information to an already-overburdened system of public education? And how were we going to make it cost-effective in a system that is constantly underfunded? How were we going to teach the teachers to incorporate even more subjects into their heavy schedules when they were already overworked? And then, how could we create a system that constantly tried to improve, reproduce and re-invent itself? We knew that we would have to heavily rely on leveraging technology.

We knew that we had to become a better filter. We had to assimilate the enormous amount of information that relates to educating a child into some sort of algorithm that could be sorted and matched easier.

We felt that igniting a child's curiosity and natural desire to learn and to achieve, needed to be our focus. And if we did it right, the process would develop the child to have a bonfire of a desire to improve their own abilities and help others to do the same, and perhaps to have it continue to grow exponentially throughout their entire lives.

Unfortunately, in education, the bureaucracy is so complex, on purpose, with special interest groups, that the mission of educating our children gets lost in various side missions to please others, including local zoning authorities, local and federal politicians, local school boards, teacher unions, parents and a multitude of other self-interest groups. Many do not have the education of children at the heart of their concern. Thus, limited funding is wasted on programs and materials that don't work, and time is wasted in dealing with issues other than meeting the needs of the students and teachers.

One of the biggest barriers in keeping education from realizing its potential or the child's has come from textbook companies. Over the past several years, textbook companies gained huge profits and market share growth, escalating into the one of largest destructive forces. Due to their own desire for profit at the expense of our children's education, they have kept all of K-12 away from developing toward learning for the twenty-first century. Heavily paired with unions and with deep pockets to pay for lobbyists, they were in back of many of the laws passed to ensure educations accountability. Textbooks were historically much more expensive than other books while everyone was mandated to have them. Textbook companies were responsible, in part, for the delay in implementing technology into schools because their lobbyists were inside of every state and national politicians offices warning of the danger of kids using technology. And they wrote white papers as expert advice to teachers about the perils of using technology with teaching or collaborating with best practice teachers. All because they wanted to control their market, no matter what happened to the kids.

As textbook companies fought hard and stealthily against the use of technology, they began losing sales of their books, anyway, so they diversified. They started getting into the technology business by developing their own student management systems. They helped No Child Left Behind to get approved requiring more rigorous testing. And guess what? They bought up nearly all of the testing companies. Even now, state required tests, given to grade school students are mostly done with pencil and paper, because the former textbook, now testing companies can control the sales better. It isn't because it is better for the teachers or kids.

In order to be considered a normal public K-12 school today, there are certain factors that must be met legally and ethically. We began to make lists of things that could be changed in education and things that could not be changed, at least for the time being.

We made lists of state, national and international standards and began to compare private schools' curricula to state standards. "If you were in charge of education reform, what would you teach in K-12 education today that would help a future forty-year-old to become a better-functioning world citizen?" After asking this question of several hundred people, the most common answers always included heritage, cultural and character development, as well as areas such as personal accountability and civic responsibility. Socratic, how-to, methodology for learning was emphasized. People suggested that students don't learn enough about the proper use of technology. Others wanted kids today to be more informed about the environment, peace-making skills and to be more engaged in their own learning. Work-study programs, entrepreneurial, business and mentoring opportunities were suggested often, as well. Art, music, physical fitness, sex education and health studies were also included in answers. People suggested that parenting classes be taught. Everyone had an opinion, some quite strong.

No wonder today's teachers are so baffled; there are opinions everywhere they cannot ignore, without a process to put them in place. Many politicians, think the students' passing of tests is the most important part of an education, due to the strong influence they receive from lobbyists representing the test-making and school textbook companies.

Our continual approach was to be as scientific as possible about how the learning process occurs and by separating and questioning each part of education without any assumptions of what it should be, other than abiding by the laws that govern education. We had to understand the learning process from as many perspectives as possible. It became obvious and sometimes daunting to find that there were many interpretations of what it means "to learn." Was learning a matter of problem-solving or mere memorization, or a combination of both influenced by other factors?

We struggled with other questions, like "What does it mean to be a school?" As obvious as this question seems, we discovered answers that became more obscure. Some speak about opening schools as if it is enough to provide a building, a teacher, some books and some students. But for the 21st century and its information explosion in a world of constant change, we felt that it was time to re-define what in fact, makes a school a school? Or, if a school is even necessary today with so many people learning on computers and phones. We wanted a school to have relevance and significance to students, teachers, parents and our country. Simply teaching a child to read today, is not going to be enough to know. In fact, reading the wrong things could and has taught many children misery.

In terms of the parts of education that cannot be changed, all states in the U.S., and in most countries, have laws that have been created to require a minimum accomplishment or level of learning at a particular age and/or grade level. There are state and national standards that have been influenced by politicians and education leaders, and there are accreditation requirements that most schools have adopted, coming originally from what universities need in prepared freshman. Accreditation insures that schools are in some agreement of a continual process of delivering a satisfactory curriculum to its students.

One of the most widely accepted and practiced forms of accreditation, nationally as well as internationally, comes from AdvanceED, an organization that "shares a unified accreditation process to help schools to continuously improve." StarShine Academy International Schools have earned accreditation from AdvanceED with North Central Accreditation as well as CITA, the Commission for International Trans-regional Accreditation.

The process for obtaining a charter public school designation differs in each state, but is commonly a long and tedious process, while kids keep struggling and parents wait. Entrepreneurs who might have wanted to get involved and help to solve the problem are diverted and in most cases encouraged to give up before they begin.

In Arizona, one of the earliest adopters for charter school laws in the United States, and considered one of the best, most progressive; the process is very complicated and can take years. Many states only allow a five-year contract, causing many education leaders to be discouraged to even begin the process, knowing most commercial leases are ten years long.

There are more consultants in education than in any other field. Consultants are an expensive part of every school's function, some charging as much as $500 for one-half hour. Many of them profess to know how to create a great education system, but they haven't done it. Consultants typically understand and can convey their particular field of expertise, but not how it all fits together with other pieces of education to create a systemic change. It is much easier to tell someone how to fix something than to have to actually do it.

The spider webs of self-serving companies that have been formed to control and prevent the improvement of schools are so thick that they have caused massive numbers of wonderful educators and political leaders to give up trying to change any of it. K-12 Education has become something for everyone else except for the kids and teachers.

Education has developed through the ages for the purpose of those doing the educating, not those needing to be educated. If a child was born into royalty, he or she was expected to learn protocol, how to work with servants, how to enjoy and participate in the arts and how to count money, among other things, and were given the teachers and resources to learn those things. A child born into an industrial community, full of factories needing workers, will most likely attend a school that endorses curricula that eventually helps those students to enter jobs in the factory.

Throughout history, our schools have not been set up to prepare individuals to be the best they can be or to help to create the world to be a better place as much as they have been in place to fulfill a specific need of industry. This focus on a specific need seemed to be satisfactory, before technology began to connect us to the entire human race in an instant. Parents and places of worship have in the past been primary in teaching children how to behave, but today share influence with many other factors. We are now in a situation of almost "too little, too late" as schools try frantically to catch up to the needs of the 21st century, but still using old designs, beliefs, memes, too-low standards and paradigms.

How to have a great life, not just how to get into college, became a strong emphasis for our discussions which resulted in an even bigger concern of how to figure out a way to integrate into schools and to teach students as well as teachers these concepts. We wanted to figure out a way to inspire (or reignite) all kids to love to learn, not merely to get by to pass a test, but to take great pride in achieving their very best, to help others along the way and to crave for more. We wanted to assimilate a way to raise and praise teachers as the great leaders that they are for the planet, probably indeed the most important ones.

We wanted to create an ironclad process that would produce the "Olympics of Education," ever improving, with everyone wanting in. We wanted to create a system that would adapt to all children regardless of talent, intelligence, background, culture or need. We were worried about our country and wanted to recapture the American Dream that was built by our Founding Fathers and influenced by our native cultures of diversity, respect and cooperation. We wanted a K-12 version of Harvard, intertwined with Behavioral Modification and Success tools.

We agreed that an educated person should contribute to the world we live in by making it a better place; to create more harmony than disharmony. We saw a school as more of a "Creative Community Learning Center" where young and old would be drawn into it. We researched and borrowed from great universities and their original missions. One of our favorite missions was from Stanford University who had two simple strategies and more than ever relevant for today:

1.   To grow cultured people and
2.   To grow useful citizens.

Can you imagine if all schools could accomplish just these two priorities, what our world might look like?

I meant only to be the coordinator and facilitator of the ideas to change education and to coordinate interested people; I had no intention of becoming an implementer. I had a background in banking and strategic design partnering, but not in public K-12 education other than as a volunteer. I knew what any parent knows about schools from that experience of raising my own children and what I read. I wanted to be some sort of catalyst for change, but only a small part.

There is a story called *"Stone Soup"* that describes how I began to see myself; about a traveler who stops to help a town that is in trouble from famine. He puts a kettle on a fire, throws a couple of stones in the water and tells the village that they are going to be able to save themselves from starving by making *"Stone Soup."* The traveler entices everyone to add their own vegetables they've been hoarding because of their fear of starving by telling them that they could have as much soup as they wanted if they helped him to prepare it. One by one, each villager begins to add what they have into the soup and soon enough they all begin to eat together. Sharing and trusting saved the people of the village.

I just wanted to create some inspiration among people I perceived as having the ability and desire to change K-12, mostly my educator friends. I was willing to set the stage for beginning the design of the soup, of redesigning education for kids. In my wildest dreams, and those of my mother's, I did not ever think that I would actually open a school myself.

TRISH MCCARTY

3

SLEEPING WITH AN EDUCATOR
MEETING DR. LEONORA KETYER

You never change things by fighting the existing reality.
To change something, build a new model that makes the existing model obsolete.
There is nothing in a caterpillar that tells you it's going to be a butterfly
--Richard Buckminster Fuller

About a year or so before I knew about and opened StarShine Academy, I was asked to deliver a speech about "Creating Strategic Partnerships" for a group of educators meeting in Flagstaff, Arizona at Northern Arizona University as a promotion for a new publication, for a chapter I had written in the Internet Encyclopedia by Wiley and Sons Publisher entitled "Strategic Alliances." The organizers had told me that we would ride in a carpool up to Northern Arizona University and that our accommodations would be provided. It seemed like an adventure to me and a day away from the world of banking, so I agreed.

When we arrived at the small, boutique hotel we went to the front desk to check in. I was told that I would be sharing a room with an esteemed educator, Dr. Leonora Farrah Ketyer. I was not used to sharing rooms with anyone other than my husband or children and never in the banking business. I gently objected, explaining that I would need my own private room. The educator woman in charge told me that we always share rooms to save money in education and I would be bunking with Dr. Leonora and that even if I could have my own room, the hotel had no other rooms available.

This was one of my first learning lessons into the world of education. I could feel my face burning and was trying hard to hide my disappointment and anger, to just go along with the flow. I could not believe educators were forced to always share rooms. Corporate executives would never be made to do this, I thought.

So I introduced myself to Dr. Leonora. She was intimidating. She was fashionable, as most educators aren't. I was told that she had opened more schools than anyone in the U.S. and that she was one of the highest paid education consultants. She had a doctorate degree and effortlessly seemed to command respect from everyone. "O.K. fine," I said in my head. Here I go.

We walked up to our little cottage room, the last one available, they said. We opened the door and much to our surprise saw one king-sized bed with a large canopy romantically covering it, and a heart-shaped Jacuzzi hot tub in the floor in front of the bed. It was the honeymoon suite. God really does have a sense of humor. "Great" I moaned. "Did you bring a swim suit?" Dr. Leonora said that she had. "I think we are going to get to know each other pretty well," I said as I walked out the door to head down the street to pick up a bottle of Champagne.

Dr. Leonora and I laughed more that night, nearly the whole night, than I have done many times in my life. She kept waking me up to tell me more things about education and to ask me about money management and the teachings of my friends, Robert and Kim Kiyosaki and their book, "Rich Dad, Poor Dad." She explained to me that all educators are financially poor and that she knew nothing about making money. I felt so sorry to hear this. Educators are the most important people on the planet. Shouldn't they have the most money?

The friendship that was formed that night became one of the most necessary for me to open a school later. At the time, it would have been the furthest thing from my mind, but it was Dr. Leonora Ketyer that caused me to actually open StarShine Academy.

Opening StarShine

'When you correct your mind, everything else falls into place.' - Lao Tzu

StarShine Academy had its own ideas for its own manifestation. It was August of 2001. I had formed a technology company and had been working on developing a large database of college scholarships with a group of investors and technology experts. Our idea was to create a matching service that would give college-bound students easier access to obtaining and being matched with appropriate scholarships. I knew something about creating matching algorithms for technology from helping to formulate one of the first interactive mortgage loan applications on the Internet. And I had become very engaged in helping education projects, mostly as a volunteer, sometimes as a strategic consultant or investor. As a part-time venture, a few years prior, I had formed my company, Education Resources, L.L.C., merely as a way to invest and provide education consultants, methods and resources for schools and government jobs. It was a way for me to try to help some aspects of education.

We had nearly completed the databases and the beta testing for the website launch, and we were gearing up with our attorneys to put together an Initial Public Offering. We had worked tirelessly on the project and had quite a bit of money tied up, so we were looking forward to making our "millions" introducing our work to the larger investment market.

One busy afternoon, my designer friend, Ann Bitters McElhinney, called me. Excitedly she said, "Trish, you have to come with me to this house in Paradise Valley tonight. Mother Mary is going to be channeled by a woman who gets regular visits from her." Even for Ann-ie who comes up with crazy things to do quite often, this was a strange phone call. "Ann," I said, "I am not Catholic and I really don't know if I believe in channeling. Besides, I am too busy and I'm not interested anyway. So I won't be going." She said, "We absolutely HAVE to go! I insist, it is going to be important!" "Oh brother," I said, "Alright, I will go with you."

Paradise Valley, Arizona is built around a lot of hills, winding streets and with large, beautiful mansions, so I was having a hard time finding the right address. As I was questioning in my mind, "Why in the world I had decided to do this?" Ann called me to tell me that she couldn't make it, but that I had to go for the two of us. Now I was starting to feel ridiculous for being talked into going with her. As I decided to turn around and go home, just then, I found the house.

It was Terri Mansfield's house, and at the time I did not think that I knew her. She answered the enormous door and with a big smile said, "You must be here to see Mother Mary! Just come on in and join the others downstairs." I felt so uneasy as I stepped down the stairs and entered a room full of complete strangers. I quietly sat down on the nearest couch that I could locate at the bottom of the stairs. I felt so conspicuous for some reason. A few minutes later, a rather sweet-looking woman took a chair directly across and facing the couch where I was sitting. Terri introduced her and she began to explain that Mother Mary had visited her and wanted to deliver messages to this group of people. I have to admit that if there had been an easy way out, I would have taken the exit, as I began to feel even more uncomfortable. The woman said some prayers and sat quietly for a few moments. Then, in a completely different voice, a softer, gentler voice, the woman began to explain that she was Mother Mary and this was a very important time for the world. And then she said, "I have a message for a person who is working for children." I felt a rush of emotion to my face and my stomach. "Surely, God, please do not let this woman be talking to me. I am not supposed to be here anyway." I said in my mind as a desperate prayer. No one spoke. Mother Mary repeated, "I must say this to the person working for children, but that person must identify themselves before I can tell them." Again, the silence was deafening. My stomach now, was in knots. I thought that it could not be me as I was working on a database and we were about to make a bunch of money. Yes, it would help kids, but not with me, directly. But after what seemed like forever, I decided to at least say, "I don't think it's me, but…" She looked deep into my eyes with a loving expression and said, "It's you." I really was so completely drained at this moment, feeling almost sick to my stomach. I was embarrassed to be in front of all of these people that I did not know, in a place I was not comfortable to be in, listening to a woman I did not know anything about. She leaned forward toward me, not taking her eyes from mine and she said, "It's not the time."

I could not believe that she said this to me. "What do you mean it's not the time?" I thought. "How could she? Why did she single me out? We are doing a wonderful thing and it is going to help everyone! And our IPO for investors is probably only days away! She can't know. She can't be right!" And then she nearly whispered, without glancing away, she said, "You are going to do great things for children throughout the world. But this one is not it. Not now." My face was burning. I wanted to cry. I wanted out of there. But Mother Mary continued to talk about love and how the world needs to learn and that everything would be ok. So I could not get up. But when her talk ended, I got up as quickly and quietly as possible, practically running, avoiding anyone who might ask me something. I did not want to talk to anybody. I was sick with emotion.

I closed the front door behind me and then I started to cry. I got into my car and thought, "God, why would you let me hear this woman? Now she has put something into my head that I can't remove and I just want it out. I know that we are doing a great thing and that it will happen and help kids everywhere to go to college."

The scholarship database was developed with partnerships from Gateway Computers, Visa, MasterCard and American Express. The servers were large and had to be kept offsite. Because of our partnership, we decided to keep them at the American Express building in New York City and had back-up servers located on different floors.

A few weeks after I met the voice of Mother Mary, her warning came true: the tragedy of 9/11 in New York City, occurred and took with it our databases. The American Express building, located in New York City was next to the Twin Towers and our servers were completely destroyed. In one day, all of our work, investments and dreams for the future were gone. Mother Mary had been right. It wasn't the time. The emotion that the world felt at that moment was about to change everything.

I, like many others, became very prayerful, trying to make sense of it all. I spent more time than ever in meditation, talking and listening to God and trying to understand how something like this tragedy could possibly have happened. I kept feeling the way that I did when I was with Michael, "If only those guys who had flown those planes knew better; if only they had been taught love rather than hate. If only their parents had been better. How are we ever going to ever fix this crazy world, driven by fear and aggression?"

That year was such an unusual year for most of us. So much was different. I cried easily. Many of us questioned our own existence and our own paths. We wondered if our children had a future. I seemed to glue myself to any story about a child suffering. I was doing a lot of public speaking at the time, to various groups mostly about business strategy, but began to interject my opinions about what the world was going to look like if we didn't start teaching children better things.

In one rather heated meeting in downtown Phoenix, I had been invited along with other business leaders to gather together to discuss the dropout problems and crime issues in Arizona. The group is called the Arizona Business and Education Coalition and was formed to try to create partnerships between business and education leaders to help support a better education system. After several minutes of discussing the poor statistics of Arizona's education system and while talking about the dropout problem, a man in the audience stood up and said, "We spend too much time talking about social rejects and unmotivated students, and all of the dropouts. We need to spend more time talking about the great kids, like my daughters, for instance, they are attending school at Harvard and they will make great leaders one day. We need to invest in the ones that have the ability to lead." I could not believe my ears. What is he thinking? Doesn't he consider that his daughters might be hurt by some kid who doesn't know any better?

Something snapped inside of me and I was compelled to jump up out of my seat, which I normally do not do. "Listen," I said, "As long as there are kids dying in our streets and as long as only some of them get a great education, rather than ALL of them, we all will share the blood on our hands! We are the leaders of this community. If it doesn't work it is our fault! We have the money, power, influence and education to fix this and yet we choose not to. It is much easier to ignore those who have no way out. Groups like this one should do more to fix these issues and talk less. Our children are dying! They must have better wisdom! WE, we must change this!" I sat down and could visualize my banking career pass away from me, as I had just made enemies with nearly everyone in that room, my friends. Then a woman in front of me began to clap, and others, one after another, joined her and for a moment, I was relieved.

When I got back to my office, I was still in shock that I had made such a spectacle of myself. Ever since the 9/11 disaster, I had become more outspoken and emotional. It seemed at times, as though I was possessed again, just like when I talked to the lady outside of Michael's school, these outbursts were not of my past character. I was embarrassed and wondered what the repercussions would be of my harsh words. As I was sitting, feeling sorry for myself, the phone rang. It was July of 2002. It was my wonderful friend, an Episcopalian priest, Rebecca McClain.

"Trish, I am going to help you to make your dreams come true. I want you to open a school. We have a run-down building in a high-crime neighborhood, where the kids need a solid education. You can use it to prove what you have always said about the very best of education being for everyone." I couldn't believe my ears! My dreams? This sounded more like a nightmare of an idea!

As she said it, I felt a lightening shock go through my body. You know about those shivers you get when you recognize something that you have never seen or someone says something to you that you remember but that you have never heard? As if I knew that it might be my destiny, the thought completely terrified me. I knew it was almost ludicrous to think of me opening a school, even though I respected Rebecca immensely and considered her a good friend, I thought that she was crazy to suggest this. I was completely unequipped to do it, not to mention the least likely, I thought. After all, I had worked in corporate America my whole life, while dabbling in various entrepreneurial ventures and continually reading and practicing yoga. I usually wore beautiful suits and pearl necklaces and earrings. My banking career was wonderful. My life was predictable. I stayed in luxury hotels and talked to important people. I felt that I was made for fixing financial problems and negotiating real estate deals. People respected my professionalism and appreciated me. I felt that my career path was set. I was making great money being "important" to my clients. And besides, my own children were nearly grown and I was looking forward to living with less worry about the day-to-day existence of my family. "This idea of opening a school has nothing to do with my background," I thought. Rebecca asked me to meet her at the proposed school site on 31st Street and Thomas in Phoenix, Arizona.

As I drove into the sad neighborhood, I started to think about how close this neighborhood was to my own in Paradise Valley, about three or four miles away, and yet worlds apart. Here was one of the highest crime neighborhoods in the United States. Mine was one of the safest. Here, kids were afraid to walk down the street and too many young girls were pregnant. The houses and yards in the neighborhood were a mess, long forgotten, any pride. Graffiti was everywhere; tagging and marking gang activity.

When I saw the San Pablo Episcopal Mission Church, a deep, sinking feeling was in my heart. The grass was nearly dead, as were several small trees. Glass was broken in windows and nothing had been painted in many years. Even the blue cross in the front had been neglected for so long, most of the paint had chipped off. I saw Rebecca drive up to meet me and just then, a small man dressed in black, I assumed to be the local priest, came out of the building, toward the parking lot with a big smile on his face and a welcoming wave.

We all exchanged hellos and walked back into the building to meet in the church's small library. The little mission on the inside did not look much better. It seemed as if everyone here was having a difficult time. The priest, though, was very excited and happy to meet me. He apologized for not being better prepared. He said that he had a rough night. "My first home I have ever owned burned to the ground last night. All I have left is one box of my things. My wife and I are blessed, though, because no one was hurt. And this is no problem, because when we came from Cuba, we only had one box of things." He gave a small laugh and looked at me with hope, "We really need a school here to help our families."

I sat there in amazement. Here is a man who just experienced devastation that most people would find permanently damaging, and he was already thinking about helping the families in the neighborhood. I almost felt ashamed that I did not have a better, easier attitude toward my own trying circumstances, certainly nothing like this man is experiencing. I knew I was not going to be able to tell him I could not help him. Rebecca was also sure of it.

He walked me through the dilapidated, former school buildings and introduced me to Maria, one of the church's volunteers, who now has been with me ever since. The rooms were filled to the ceiling of old clothes and trash, stored for some reason, but holding black widow spiders, cockroaches and mice, who had been in residence for years. Tears continually welled-up in my eyes, sometimes feeling sorry for this neighborhood and sometimes due to my own fears and feeling scared for myself. I left this place that day and felt that my life was going to dramatically change whether or not I wanted it to.

I called my best business advisor, my mom, Ruby Sanders, in Durango, Colorado on the phone and told her what Rebecca had said and I started to cry. "She wants me to open a school, Mom, on the worst drive-by shooting street. I can't do it. I don't know how. I could get sued."

My mom has always been my most savvy business advisor because she is so intuitive, but this time I wasn't so sure. She said, "Oh Patricia, you'll be okay, you're probably just in 'a calling' and God will take care of you. If you're not supposed to do it, you will know. If it's that bad of a neighborhood, you can't make it much worse. If you make a bunch of mistakes, it won't matter because they are already shooting each other in the neighborhood. Just do the best you can. I am sure that you will get all of the help that you need. And Tricia, if it is a calling, there is nothing you can do to stop it."

My mom said something that day, I think is one of the best pieces of advice all of us need to remember when things get tough. Mom said, "Just put one foot in front of the next. That's all. You don't need to see past where your car headlights are showing you. None of us knows what's around the corner, anyway." Buckminster Fuller says that, "There are no geniuses, just people who had good mothers."

I knew in this moment, I was in a calling and it was going to happen whether or not I was ready, but I certainly didn't feel prepared or even qualified to be the head of a school. After all, my whole training had been in finance and business, not education. However, I knew someone who was qualified, my friend, Dr. Leonora Farrah Ketyer. She was more than qualified and I was sure if I called her she would love to have her own school. I would just help her.

After Rebecca convinced me, along with Mom, that I would be in the business of schools, I made a decision that I would just offer to help someone to establish their own school, someone like Leonora or maybe another educator who had always wanted their own school.

Leonora was the perfect blend of passion and expertise. Who better to run a school? Relieved at thinking of having the burden lifted from my shoulders, I called Leonora. But when I called her, Leonora didn't share my vision of her as Director of a new school in the San Pablo Mission Church.

When I reached Leonora and told her what was going on, I asked her if she would like for me to help her to have her own school. She told me that no amount of money would get her to open a school on what was then, the worst drive-by shooting street, but if I was going to do it, she would help. I figured that we might be able to find someone else to come along as the director later. I also figured that it would take at least one year of planning to start to make the school a reality. I had been working a lot of hours and coupled with this new idea, decided to take some time off. I told Leonora that I was going to go to Hawaii for a couple of weeks and when I got back we would start to work on the school.

Leonora heard the "couple of weeks" part and while I was gone vacationing in Hawaii, went through the violent neighborhood telling families that we were going to open a new school in a few weeks, on Sept. 3, 2002. When I got off of the plane on August 16th there was a message on my phone from Leonora explaining that she had 28 kids signed up and ready to attend school in two weeks...

StarShine Opened

"Teach a child a lesson, he will learn. Teach a child how to love learning, and he will enlighten the world."

I walked up the partially broken sidewalk toward a building that looked like it had been through a lot of turmoil in its sixty years. As I looked at the scene before me, my stomach hurt; I had butterflies in it and I felt sick. "What in the world am I doing here?" I thought. But then I caught a glimpse of Dr. Leonora Ketyer cheerfully standing near a table tied with balloons, where she was trying to talk to parents who could not understand English so that they could enroll their children into the new school. I could see the apprehension in their faces, the worry of having experienced disappointment so many times and in so many schools before, and I could also see the light of hope in their eyes that this school might be different, the one that they had been praying for, so that their children could have advantages that their parents never did.

I could hardly believe that I was there. Never in my wildest dreams would I have thought that I would open a school at all, but particularly a school for children destined to be among the failures of our society. These were the "throwaway kids" the ones that some might say didn't really matter. Most people from my neighborhood described them as uninspiring, dangerous and a menace to our country. Others just said that they were transparent and that since they would never amount to much, and we couldn't change their unfortunate lot in life, we could just ignore them, and leave them to their own demise. "Some people are just luckier than others," they would say. I never thought this way; my parents used to tell me that to whom much is given, much is required; to be thankful for what I have and to share.

Mothers, who have been told as young children that they will never amount to much, usually don't. And unfortunately, as much as they want their children to have more (I am convinced all mothers love their children,) they feel unable to help them. They don't know what they don't know. People that have been constantly made to feel insignificant usually feel powerless and victimized by everything. "No shame, blame, victim, allowed," my parents would say and today this is a central theme for us at StarShine, as we work to give power back to students and their teachers.

Just as I was about to help Leonora and another volunteer philanthropic friend, Susan French, try to arrange paperwork, I was abruptly approached by what would be the beginning of a long series of bureaucratic heavy-handedness that continually interferes in our schools' ability to provide children access to what they need.

"Mrs. McCarty," a woman said, "I am from the Fire Marshall's office. Your fire alarms are inadequate and I cannot let you open the school today." I am fairly adept at paying attention to rules and being compliant with laws, as this is a regular day in banking, so I had filed the necessary paperwork and attended the appropriate zoning meetings. I calmly told her that we had fire alarms that had been previously inspected, we had the appropriate paperwork filed and we had a completely block concrete building and each classroom had two doors to the outside for adequate release of the students, should there be an emergency.

She looked at me with an intense flash of anger in her face as if to say that I had no right to question her authority in this matter, obviously astounded that I could disagree with her position. She quickly and sternly informed me, "I will not argue with you, Mrs. McCarty. You are violating the law and I will not allow these children to attend this school today." She held her clipboard tightly to her chest as if it was armor. "What is the mission here?" I thought, "Is she helping the kids to safety or protecting her turf? Because if we turn these kids back out on the street, they will not be safe."

I did what we teach the kids to do, I slowed my breathing to deep breathing, I lifted one foot off of the ground to cause me to hold my balance, which helps to balance the brain and stop anger or fear. I glanced around and could see the excitement in the eyes of the children, dressed and ready for a new adventure. Time for a moment, became very slow as I saw the loving, hopeful look on the faces of the parents as they watched their children, hoping for a new beginning for their family.

I took a deeper breath and did something else out of character. "I'm sorry for the misunderstanding and inconvenience to you," I said, "You see we're not opening a school today. These children are all my cousins, nieces and nephews and I have to babysit." I caught her off guard. She wrote out a little pink slip off of her clipboard, tore it off and handed it to me as she quickly told me that she would return in thirty days to inspect a new fire alarm.

That cost to me was $12,000, unbudgeted, but it is still one of my favorite stories about the hardships of trying to do something good for society. Unfortunately, I have a myriad of these types of stories from the past many years of opening schools, because for whatever reason many of the people in positions that could have helped me care for the kids, chose instead to be against what I was trying to do. Maybe they thought that the school project and philosophies were too unrealistic and overly unattainable, destined to fail. Some surely thought that I was crazy and would waste my time and my money, and never make a difference. Maybe they were all trying to save me from making a mistake.

The location for StarShine's first school was on a known violent street, a part of the outreach mission church for the Episcopal Diocese in Arizona. The school building attached to the church had not been used in years. It was a mess of broken windows, graffiti and old stored clothes and materials. All of the grass had died and even the bushes were struggling. Trash was everywhere. The neighborhood was completely overrun with gangs, shootings, and drug deals, and the adjacent neighbors' yards seemed to have given up long ago. But the Episcopal Church at that time, particularly the Very Reverend Rebecca McClain, believed in our dream and ability (more than we did at that time) and wanted to help establish a school for the families in the neighborhood.

When we opened the first StarShine Academy, nothing made much sense, or so it seemed. I was the leader, without an education background. The only money we had was the money in my personal accounts and credit cards. The area was considered the most-violent-crime zip code in Arizona, full of kids who didn't seem to want to be in school, some even had guns. The buildings were a mess. The air conditioners didn't work, and it was 110 degrees in the shade. The roofs and ceilings all leaked, and the monsoon season was beginning to peak. There was no play equipment. All of the classrooms were completely full of old clothes, trash, cockroaches, black widow spiders and mice that had all been dripped on from the leaking ceilings for years. It was pretty disgusting and very discouraging.

But people started showing up to help. Maria Murillo was the very first angel. She had been attending and volunteering with the adjacent Episcopal Church with her family, praying for a school to open. She needed money but was willing to work for free just to help realize her dream for her children to attend a safe school. She and I called everyone we knew, and they came to help.

My designer friend, Ann Bitters McElhinney, showed up in shorts with spray cans of paint and began to create a beautiful scene of mountains, water and palm trees on the side of one of the ugly buildings. She painted all day, every day, for days in the scorching sun, (it was averaging 112 degrees) just to do her part, as one of the little boys kept bringing her wet towels to put on her forehead to cool off. And then a huge miracle occurred: The word about the school's opening inspired some community leaders to get involved.

Valley Partnership, comprised of nearly 1000 Phoenix community leaders in real estate development, chose StarShine for their community project as a "Creative Community Barn-Raising." It was orchestrated and managed so well, when over 500 volunteers showed up on Saturday morning in November, they were given different-colored tee shirts that designated the area that they would work in. In five and one-half hours, the dirt, messes and garbage were transformed to grass and full-grown trees with a beautiful playground, basketball court and school. Carpet was installed, air conditioners were donated and everything was painted. People came to help. There were old people and young people, firemen and gangsters, CEOs and artists. Muzak broadcasted music throughout the school, Starbucks donated coffee, and The Duck and Decanter Restaurant donated sandwiches.

Even today, when I think back on that experience of watching so many dedicated and diverse people, working toward a common community good, the vision catches my breath, and I get tears in my eyes. Vernon Swaback, our board member and also a friend and my mentor, summed it up in his typically-eloquent way: "As I look out across these grounds and watch the people as if they are all designated colored ants, no one getting out of line, all working for one common theme, I witness the magnificence of the human potential to do good together, and it gives me hope for the future. This is the most beautiful symphony I have ever seen." On that day, a community built a cathedral, one that creates harmonious sound, beauty and hope for all who enter.

The students attending the first StarShine came from very tough situations, typically. There were some families that had fewer struggles but gang and illegal activity had influenced most of the children. Shootings, stabbings and drug use was prevalent in many of the families. They were truly "victims" of terrible circumstances. We brought together neighborhood groups to talk with them to find out what they wanted. We told them that we had a limited time each day during school in order to help them toward a better life. We said that we could spend each day talking about all of the terrible things that happened the day before and try to understand, or we could focus efforts on how they could learn to produce lives that they wanted. They chose the latter. So we borrowed my families' saying that has changed all of us, "No shame, blame, or victim here." We each take responsibility for creating a future we want and do everything possible to leave the past behind. The students and teachers remind themselves of that motto daily as it helps them to stay focused and pro-active in creating their better future instead of re-living past disappointments.

As human beings, we spend over ninety percent of our time thinking about history. We continually visualize past disappointments or bad news. We relive ancient hurts. We hold on to fear. We are a nation of victim thinking, and it is a very powerful drug. It undermines everything and continually re-creates itself.

StarShine is a living example and proof that what you think about you bring about. It makes sense to think more about how you WANT things to be rather than what you DON'T want. And yet it seems to elude most of us, much of the time. It is not an easy habit to cultivate positive thinking. We are continually bombarded by negative information from the radio, the news, listening to people talk to one another or television. It affects the playback messages in our mind and keeps us in a continually negative mood. Always looking for good or what is right and building on that, rather than complaining about what is wrong and compiling statistics on that, is imperative to those who seek success of any kind.

StarShine is managed with StarShine Guiding Principles; to organize and run by mutual agreement, rather than by rules of control and intimidation. Later in this book, I will discuss these in detail and how our students, parents and volunteers observe them.

When I started to talk to officials about opening a charter school, I was told that I did not belong in the business of schools as I was not educated as a school administrator. They apparently were not seeking any new ideas or ready to support someone bringing any new thought to their problems. One formidable woman in the Arizona Department of Education said that she would do all she could to prevent me from being able to open a school. I said, "I am a nice person with a great management background and I can hire educators. I am trying to help." And she did everything she could to get me to go away. Time after time, she refused to help us and at times was sarcastic and rude. This type of behavior was and still is more of the "norm" in education bureaucracy. New ideas and entrepreneurial spirit are frowned upon in most education circles. I found out later that this particular woman had earlier been involved in opening a charter school that failed. So how did she get her job?

Needless to say, they didn't make it easy for me. It took three tries of getting turned down for me to obtain our own charter. They thought the garden would waste student learning time. They were totally against putting K-12 together. I told them they would help one another and they do. They thought teaching kids international protocol was a joke. Basically, they just did not want my school ideas there. But some did.

Prior to getting our own charter, we had to operate under the umbrella of other charter schools to keep our doors open and to remain "legal." I had to financially support the school because there was no money coming in other than a few donations from friends. It was extremely stressful and complicated for us. There was no best practice to follow. I even hired a Superintendent from Alaska to fly down to help me with some school management ideas because I read about some of his work. He had won the first Malcolm Baldrige Award for Excellence for Education and I thought he could help to give me a good start.

I believed that schools should reflect what society and the surrounding community needs and I believed and had to prove that all grades together, K-12 all in one school, was the best way for kids to learn. You can imagine my stress level of trying to learn about all of the legal requirements that must be met to teach thirteen grades while also having to learn the governing and political system at the same time, while also running a school full of a bunch of children with high needs.

I learned that Arizona is one of the most forward-thinking states in many ways, even though national news likes to say otherwise. There are many state legislators and those in the Arizona Department of Education who are dedicated to making Arizona schools be the best in the country. But the system overall is a mess. Fear and distrust has formed systems upon systems that do not work locally, nationally or internationally, and never have, yet they continue to stay in place. Arizona has one of the worst funding resources for education so I figured if I could make the school work within the budget suggested by Arizona, it had a chance to work anywhere.

Businesses are continually nurtured to open in towns and cities across America. Groups are in place to assist businesses in determining their locations and representatives for economic departments try to find businesses willing to open in their respective cities. Most businesses are encouraged to open and many resources exist to enable them to prosper. Entrepreneurs are praised for their bravery and their determination to provide jobs for the public. You would think if someone wanted to open a great school, they would be supported for increasing economic development. Almost everyone knows that one of the leading reasons people take or don't take jobs in a particular place is because of their children's' school needs and choices.

Almost the opposite is true in education. Just mentioning that a new school might be opening causes eyebrows to rise, questions to be drilled and sometimes, anger to be released. An entrepreneur like I am, wanting to help, is frowned upon as if education should not be thought of as entrepreneurial. And discouragement is everywhere, from kids to teachers to departments of education. In too many states people in education departments refuse to answer questions about how to open a new school. You will be referred to department websites where the state's department of education usually has a Frequently Asked Questions page about how to open a school. Vague answers are posted to questions and for further information, you can request a returned call by email. Typically there is only one time period per year allowed to apply to open a new charter school and it is different in every state.

One cutoff date is for a Letter of Inquiry stating that you intend to open a school and one other date is a final date whereby you must submit a very lengthy charter application. Missing either dates will cause you to have to wait another year. But submitting the material on time does not guarantee that you will be allowed to open a school. And if you are able to get through all of the determination periods with a positive outcome and a final approval to open a charter school, you won't be allowed to open until the following beginning of the next school year, over one year from receiving your final approval. And many states now have adopted a five-year limit to a charter license, meaning that it could take up to three years to receive an approval for a five-year license, which you have to reapply to receive an extension for, and there are no guarantees. Most businesses cannot negotiate leases or bank loans if they are only allowed to be in business for five years. But these are the perils that face anyone wanting to try to help kids by opening community charter schools. It is as if they hope you don't. This is one reason people don't even try, even when they might be able to provide an outstanding school for kids.

The process is daunting and it is for people inside of the education departments as well. The paperwork for everyone is overwhelming and the system is not fair, especially if you consider that we are all trying to find better, easier ways to educate our nation's children. People scoring the charter applications are usually not very creative in assessing any new education ideas, one reason so many are turned down. The status-quo is maintained because the system makes it so difficult to try to change.

Lack of resources sometimes causes great creativity and it did at StarShine. Lack of enough funding for StarShine forced all of us to work constantly toward creating a design for an extremely effective and efficient system. We had to continually learn how to have much more with much less. I had used my own funds, making it more of a priority never to allow any money or time to waste. The systems and curriculums we developed had to be cutting edge to obtain better student outcomes with smaller per-student costs or it would not have worked.

I studied several private schools that operate efficiently with a much smaller per-student cost than most large public schools and yet they, many times are better at educating students. We dissected every cost/efficiency ratio that we could find. And we leveraged technology whenever possible without forfeiting important human relationship learning. What we accomplished could not have been done in years past. With technology students and teachers have greater, available resources at the touch of their hands for a small cost.

It would be nearly impossible to produce true *Individualized Learning Plans* for every student without utilizing technology to support our teachers. In too many schools, the technology available is not efficiently used. The vast majority of schools still use "technology labs" as if technology belongs in its own category. StarShine uses any available technology, including smart phones, as if they are a pencil. Technology assists learning all of the time. We cannot separate technology from tasks at schools any longer if we are to grow citizens compatible with the changes that will be demanded of the future.

I did not borrow any money until 2010, when state budgets for schools began to plummet, and even then paid it back right away. Debt is expensive and can begin to cause managers to make decisions that are not in the best interest of their mission. For the first time ever in my life, I had to lay-off workers because of inadequate state funding in 2010. Some of the teachers had been with me for eight years. It was a devastating and stressful time for all innovative charter schools as well as district schools. During that year, schools across the nation closed. The majority of them were in severe-need neighborhoods. When kids in tough neighborhoods lose their schools, due to school closure, even not so great schools, it causes them to lose the last straw of trust they have with society and typically they do not re-enroll in other schools afterward. This year was so stressful it caused Jan Shoop, our principal and my strongest supporter, to become ill, forcing her to go on a medical leave of absence. I didn't know if I could withstand it.

Several times I have been asked why, with such a worthy project, we did not receive funding from Bill Gates, or Oprah. Maybe it was because I make everyone come to see the kids if they donate to us. But when we were struggling to pay bills and to keep the doors opened, it would have been wonderful to suddenly have received a great funding check in the mail, but it may have caused us to lose the momentum that comes from building something great from nothing but love, devotion and creativity. Most of the people that caused StarShine to become the StarShine of today were not paid at all or were severely underpaid. For example, Scott Lerman designed, developed and paid for our first brochure where I demanded that he include a short explanation, "This brochure was done for love, not money by Scott Lerman of Lucid Brands."

4

TECHNOLOGY
COMPUTERS, BRAINS AND PROCESSES

It has become appallingly obvious that our technology has exceeded our humanity. ~Albert Einstein

Our world has become complicated, and yet we continue to operate it as if we were living one hundred years ago, only now we have triple lives; one for Facebook, one for emails and one we do with other people. We have piled up so many things to do with only a moment in time to do them, yet we have not come up with a different way to do things. We multi-task and think it is effective. (Brain researchers tell us that this is not the case.) We talk while we are typing e-mails, while we are looking up Facebook, while we are updating on Twitter and while we are driving! By the end of the day, we are exhausted and can't even remember many of the things that we did. Our interpersonal relationships suffer, in fact too many of us feel as if we don't have any real relationships anymore. We remind ourselves that somewhere, someone said "Stop and smell the roses," but we laugh because we can't remember when. This is happening to all of us exponentially, as we were unprepared to live in the world that we now have. We are now in a crisis, trying to figure out what is going to work to better prepare our children.

The learning crisis is the worst for kids. In his book *The Dumbest Generation*, Mark Bauerlein talks about the bombardment of advertising on our children and their thirst for instant gratification that leads to disempowerment and depression and to a brain that labors with dysfunction. He talks about children today growing up with more technology, more knowledge around them and more visits to museums, and yet they are less inquisitive, less knowledgeable and less responsible than at any time in history. He writes about their social connectedness but lack of social skills to get along with one another or their elders.

If children were better-informed consumers, they would have fired the status quo system a long time ago. As customers, they certainly have not obtained what they were buying, a sound education system to prepare them for a successful life. Sam Walton said, "There is only one boss. The customer. And he can fire everybody in the company from the chairman on down, simply by spending his money somewhere else." Of course, kids couldn't fire their schools or their parents. They have been stuck receiving whatever was given out to them, whether it helped or hurt them. And it has cost a lot of money. The kids have had too small of a voice to be heard. Their parents did not know how to fire the system either, as the government has continued to tell them what they were going to get and how they were going to get it, driven by pure-profit motivated lobbying groups instead of what was right.

Wealthy parents in many towns across the U.S. simply started their own private schools for their own children, with their own criteria for what they thought their children needed to become educated. Churches did the same thing. But because these groups had to learn along the way, as no established great system had evolved, they too made costly mistakes with the kids. But underprivileged kids and their neighborhoods have been the most neglected for having to "buy" what ever was there, without much in choice.

We wanted to design an education system that would allow for greater efficiency, so we spent a great deal of time learning about learning, and how it happens. We watched and talked to the kids in our own petri dish. We needed to filter the most important student needs to the top of the pile. This led us to design a learning system that would support the "whole" child: Body, mind, spirit, health, wealth and happiness. The extensive research that we found in brain learning processes with leading scientists, physicians and researchers created practices that demonstrate effective and efficient training for children and adults. We wanted to work *"with"* the body and brain, rather than try to get the body and brain to conform to what we wanted to accomplish, as schools and businesses traditionally have been set up to do. And we wanted to design an education system to support the needs of the community, parents, teachers and children, rather than fit all of them into the needs of the school.

As we learned about how the brain learns, we realized that present-day classrooms are designed almost completely *opposite* to how students need to learn. According to the book *Brain Rules*, Dr. John Medina, a brain-research scientist writes that a typical classroom today actually turns a student's brain off, so it takes much more time and effort to learn something. If we wanted to teach the students more in the same amount of time, we needed to make sure to keep a student's brain on and tuned-in.

The longer a person sits still, for example, the quicker his or her brain starts to shut down and to wander. If a boring lecture is being given, too often true in current education classes, the results are counter-productive for the students, not to mention how tired and burned-out this environment makes the instructors. "Interweaving" or what StarShine calls "themed learning," maximizes our student's ability to learn any subject by relating it to another. Simply studying one subject for one hour and then going to the next one in the next hour is a much less effective way to learn something, so StarShine usually does not do it. Mixing up the environments in which a student learns something is also a brain-stimulating learning tool. Music makes you smarter. Meditation stimulates brain cell reproduction. Dance is used at StarShine as is art, chess, foreign language and juggling, all to enhance brain-learning. We use cutting edge brain-developing software that the kids think are games.

Brain-based learning, however, is only one aspect of the StarShine (and any good) learning system. Individual filters, and our worldviews, that drive our perceptions and beliefs, determine how we learn as well. Some views may be based on our assumptions, while others are driven by our personalities. The total sum of our previous experiences filters our ability to allow new information in. *Memes,* a word similar to genes, are discussed at length in Richard Brodie's book, *Virus of the Mind,* suggesting that ideas transferred from another person's opinion, can become so deeply embedded in our own mind that they might have an effect on DNA. They become the beliefs of entire cultures.

I watched an interview on television with *Three Cups of Tea* author, Greg Mortenson, as he explained that the military in Afghanistan continue to think that dropping bombs is going to bring peace, but the elders there know that it won't. Culturally and structurally the environment is not set up to allow a forced violent change. The more violent the bombings, the more determined the opposition. It is another example of people operating with the wrong information. They don't know what they don't know, so they continue to think that they are right.

As we delved deeper into this question about how learning actually happens, we began to get more excited about the work that we were to do. There seemed to be a vast territory of possibilities that had never been tried. In serendipity, I found a book from the seventies entitled *In Search of Significance* as I was cleaning out a bookshelf where my husband had stored many of his old college textbooks. In the midst of an ocean of dusty books that had landed on the floor, I sat for hours completely spellbound by the information in this book that had been written so long ago. It was as if the author, Dr. Jack Brennecke, had the vision similar to StarShine back in the seventies. I became so excited by this discovery that I spent the next several weeks tracking him down. When I finally found him, we shared passion as we spoke on the phone of our desire to make the realm of education more significant and fantastic. He said that, although the book had not sold many copies, it was still a favorite of his and many of his students. We are in the process of re-publishing the book and re-launching Jack's dream, as the information contained is timeless. It was his particular writings about Maslow's Hierarchy that became the basis of how we started to create and evaluate the StarShine curriculum.

Abraham Maslow designed Maslow's Hierarchy in 1943 in a paper he wrote about his theory of motivation. It has been adopted worldwide as a simple, yet sophisticated way to understand why or what motivates us and how we can change it. Often explained as a pyramid, with the bottom driver being food, then safety and security, next love and belonging, then self-esteem and confidence and only then will you become creative and spontaneous and trusting. Every college teaches Maslow's Hierarchy, but almost no one uses it in practical application. If every person thought about it or talked about it with their friends or families, or every company discussed it with their employees, or every school required teachers to observe students and apply help according to Maslow's, everything would work better. We would see a difference.

When I first became directly involved with education, it seemed common sense that we all, educators, would not attempt to "teach" a child who was hungry or angry; we would need to address those things first. But as StarShine began to develop and interact with many hundreds of other schools, I realized this strategy was highly unique to StarShine. Eventually, this became a mainstay theme and today is one of our Fifteen Guiding Principles.

If you are hungry, angry, lonely or tired…don't talk or do anything with anyone else; you will mess things up. Take care of yourself first (like on the plane…put oxygen on yourself first so everyone doesn't die)…this is called **HALT**: Hungry, Angry, Lonely, or Tired? **HALT!** And this is how we work with our kids and teachers. If only parents…all adults would incorporate this into their behavior, our world would be a different place, and this all relates to the brain and its ability to function.

The easiest way to incorporate HALT or Maslow's Hierarchy as a means to more easily navigate life is to check yourself: How do you feel? Why? Maybe you should take a nap or get some food. But whatever you do, don't try to have a meaningful discussion when you aren't feeling at the top of your game. And when your children are crabby, don't judge them, get curious. Ask them if they are hungry. Or ask them if they had a hard time at school today. Or ask them if they need some attention. Nearly all anger or outbursts are due to something else. So the next time you feel like blaming someone for making you feel bad, try not to take it personally. The other person is most likely having a bad day, or a bad hour and you might be able to help them to turn things around, if you stay calm and caring.

All of us at StarShine have gone to great lengths to come up with ideas to outperform standards for education, adopted for schools. While most schools concentrate on what a student learns, StarShine's focus is to help the student to understand why and how they learn. State or international standards are only a starting place for what we want the kids to know. The culture that StarShine developed because of this focus is the primary cause of StarShine's incredible success. *Culture is everything.* Our success has caught the attention of many critical eyes in the field of learning. Rigorous documentation and analysis has been required to prove our processes and validate our expanded student data.

StarShine adopted many philosophies to create its success. Two of these are KISS, "KISS, Keep It Simple and Significant" and WOW, "World of Wonderful," These simple ideas have helped to continually watch for easier, simpler and more cost effective ways to implement change. Also, we do not change without a considerable amount of thought; convinced that the change will add an eighty-percent or more improvement or we wait until it will. And in everything we do we want to achieve a "WOW."

Much later, toward 2008, as we began to frame a business system around a blended co-op/franchise network, an idea for a profitable and effective support system for excellence, began to emerge. We began to consider ways to make available what we had learned to a larger audience for a faster adoption. We wanted to save as many kids as possible. Our proprietary process to guarantee accreditation standards and align matching materials, tools and curriculum to standards required by AdvancEd, North Central Accreditation, the Commission for International Transregional Accreditation, Career Tech Ed Business Management, the U.S. Core Standards and International Baccalaureate Standards have caused enormous support for our network.

Last night I attended a social function and was introduced to a rather distinguished-looking, well-educated woman from the East Coast, a member of one of the wealthiest families of historical United States who seemed almost sad as she asked me, "Do you think public education in the U.S. is ever going to be saved?" I responded to her by explaining that charter schools are public schools, just a bit more entrepreneurial in how they run, especially in how they put their boards together. In too many large districts, for too many years, the local teachers and administrators have had to put up with cantankerous governing boards, elected by the public, and as a stepping-stone toward aspiring to running for political offices. The money and the help for teachers and students is wasted at the top in unproductive bureaucracy and over-controlling boards and never reaches the classrooms needing the help.

If all schools became charter schools and the superintendent or business manager could choose board members, like most corporations, based on their ability to provide expertise and help, public education would be immediately changed forever, and might possibly work for every child and every teacher. Boards would then be in place to support and focus on the needs of the schools, rather than their individual political careers. School boards are notorious for causing superintendents and principals huge headaches as they try to force their personal agendas on mostly sweet people trying to take care of kids.

TRISH MCCARTY

5

KISS: WHAT DIFFERENCE DOES STARSHINE MAKE

"We are what we love, not what loves us."
Charlie Kaufman, *Adaptation*

StarShine kids and staff are taught executive protocol; the things taught to AT&T and Motorola executives about how to express themselves appropriately. There are Executive Protocol firms and positions in government. When I was a young executive, I went to classes to learn about proper handshakes, proper dress and introductions and appropriate conversation when visiting other nations. I remember wondering why this kind of learning was not taught in our schools, even in my early twenties.

"Most of our younger, and many of our older employees, are not prepared to properly represent themselves or our company in certain business and social settings. Simply put, they do not know what they do not know."
--Chuck Rawley, Chief Development Officer, YUM! Brands,

When you walk onto a StarShine campus, students walk directly up to you and they extend their hand in a friendly, confident way to introduce themselves to you. Many times, our kindergarteners have made adults cry as they seem so caring and strong. The students learn to appropriately look at someone with direct eye contact and they learn about the cultural rules that surround that protocol. They learn proper eating and table manners. They learn to cook food and serve one another.

We search for the most sophisticated business practices that could be modified and taught to children, giving them enormous advantage toward their future successes. But it also gives them a great way to become proud of their own behaviors and to notice inappropriate behavior more easily.

Recently, the same official, less than supportive, woman-in-charge from the Department of Education who has always given us a hard time, ridiculed me for teaching the kids "Executive Protocol" saying that our motivation in teaching the kids to shake hands was simply to "show off" but that "although cute" she said, it did not impress her one bit and in fact, made her know for sure that we weren't concentrating on the basics of an academic education. As always, I had to bite my tongue to keep from saying anything that might get us into trouble. But I am sure most of you reading this book will agree with me...how did these people get to be in charge of our education system?

The StarShine schools have a unique and happy hummmm. For a while, we didn't notice. But we have made it a priority to visit other schools as often as possible to try to learn anything we can about improving. After several visits to other schools, we all had a similar observance: other schools' kids made louder, more aggressive noises. After discussing this at length and becoming more aware of other school campuses we could see a profound difference in the behaviors related to sound. More helpful kids and teachers create a more harmonious sound and more laughter. Bullying and laughing at someone has a louder, more obnoxious sound. And engaged students and teachers make almost no sound at all. Even first-time visitors have remarked at how quiet the campus seems. This is the outcome of developing a strong, positive culture of engaged learning.

In every classroom you will notice technology. Some kids are using phones for their work, some students are on computers, some groups are with a teacher and others are groups of students working with an Electronic White Board. Sometimes it isn't evident of who is doing the teaching, because as one of our Guiding Principles states, "All students are teachers and all teachers are students."

A focus on music and the arts are evident throughout the campuses as you can see students performing and can hear classical or rock music playing. Sculpture and beauty is everywhere, as is nature and gardening. We have always said that schools should look like the imagination of Disneyland and Las Vegas, combined with the magic in the world of Narnia if we really want to inspire kids and their brains. And the teachers need to be entertainers with the personality of Disneyland employees, not boring government workers. We cannot regulate teachers into being great. We need to help, encourage, train and allow them to be all they can be. We must make learning the best thing on the planet to do, because it is. Our future depends on our own ability to do rapid learning.

Our schools focus on the environment and our responsibility to live more "Green" lives, not only in our surroundings but with regard to the students' own bodies. Sustainability is 75% behavioral. They learn about how important food and energy is to their bodies and to the earth through participating in the community gardening program. And all of the students must be engaged in helping the local community with various service projects. Our kindergarten classes each year, every day collects, weigh and distribute food for the homeless and poor. As StarShine continues to grow and expand to more schools, a greater emphasis on creating sustainable schools and communities will be evident.

Business mentors are typically on our campuses, as we require that every high school student learn something as an apprentice. So each student has one or more mentors. And when we can find them, we ask businesses to adopt the younger classrooms as well. Learning by doing is the most efficient way to learn anything and lasts the longest. Everyone at StarShine, including the teachers must have dreams and goals

Our rule since the beginning for making decisions has always been "KISS; Keep It Simple and Significant," one that I learned while working at AT&T. If a change in practice does not lead to an 80% gain in student or teacher performance, we don't integrate it until it does. One of the most difficult things for people in an organization to work with is another "good idea" from another well-intentioned supervisor. We work through a company-wide agreement process and only then, implement it. This becomes a very expeditious, relevant way to make systemic change. We aren't changing with the wind, but if storms come, we can adapt quickly. Changes today, whether in large or small corporations have critical timing requirements, so people must be ready to implement a crucial change, but to make changes too often, confuses everyone and creates an inefficient system.

StarShine has changed very little from its first organizational mission and business plan; the focus is still to be the leading change agent for education for every K-12 child on the planet; to bring the best resources in the most efficient way to every child. Every person, including the students are empowered and encouraged to improve it.

Many people wondered why we felt that it was so important to change the approach to the way children learn. By virtue of our never-ending thirst to acquire more data, students have to be able to learn more efficiently, more meaningful learning within a shorter length of time. It is important that we begin to raise citizens who are not only brilliant, but are kind, compassionate, responsible to the greater good, who possess integrity, social skills, and the ability to disagree with understanding, if we are to survive as a society. Students also must learn how to be very self-disciplined in order to design their own lives in healthy ways. With anything positive or negative within the reach of a home computer, we must learn ways to make empowering decisions. Students and teachers need to know how to prioritize information and duties like no other time in history. Being able to find and implement information that we need, becomes more of an issue as the Internet continues to grow. These things can be taught.

As we began to observe and codify the results that we were seeing in the StarShine students, amazing things began to happen. The students began to act as if they were in charge. Students were correcting one another, picking up trash, opening doors for teachers and asking for more time in the garden. Pushing, fighting, talking back to teachers, not showing up for class, all seemed to be disappearing. The school was full of kids who had dropped out of school, flunked previous classes, and had come from trouble, and yet now we observed students who just wanted to please us. For many of these children, this was probably the first time they had ever experienced respect from adults.

We began to notice what love and respect could do. Every day the students were teaching us what we didn't know. It became glaringly obvious to me that the most important things that we all learn are not necessarily those things that can easily be memorized. Instead, some of the most important lessons come from the practice of doing. They are lessons that are so integrated into muscle memory that they become a part of our life. We learn how to love ourselves so that we can love others better.

TRISH MCCARTY

6

THE WOW FACTOR: WHAT MAKES STARSHINE DIFFERENT?

"Benefit is the end of nature. But for every benefit which you receive, a tax is levied. He is great who confers the most benefits. He is base,—and that is the one base thing in the universe,—to receive favors and render none. In the order of nature we cannot render benefits to those from whom we receive them, or only seldom. But the benefit we receive must be rendered again, line for line, deed for deed, cent for cent, to somebody. Beware of too much good staying in your hand. It will fast corrupt and worm worms. Pay it away quickly in some sort. -Emerson on Compensation

There is a little restaurant in Tucson, Arizona called Café Poca Cosa *"The Little Thing."* This is written on their website: "The menu which changes twice daily is written in English and Spanish (in perfect longhand) on a portable chalkboard, which servers take from table to table. This fun spontaneous approach to dining encourages guests to sample old favorites and to discover new ones." Suzana Davila's artistic cooking comes from her original Sonora, Mexico roots. When Suzana told the (mostly male) chefs in Mexico that she would one day have one of the best restaurants in the United States, everyone made fun of her. But today she is celebrated worldwide as one of the best chefs, especially of Mexican cuisine. My husband and I believe it is one of the best restaurants we have been to. It isn't only the food, which is fantastic; it's the *"little things."* Every detail, from the way the servers treat you to the beautiful art on the walls, to the chalkboards, is meant to make you say "WOW."

StarShine students and teachers are taught to be always outstanding, exhibit and look for the "WOW, World of Wonderful" in everything. They represent "WOW" in how they look, how they act and what they experience. StarShine students, teachers and staff want to be examples of doing the unexpected, even in *the little things*, all of the time, to "WOW" someone, to give more than what is expected, to want to do the greatest thing in that moment, to cause a smile, a laugh or a huge thank-you.

StarShine teaches that your life is the only one you have, so you might want to choose to live at the best level possible in each moment. We surround ourselves with "OQP" Only Quality People. Whomever or whatever you continually think about, any person, real or imaginary, will have a profound effect on you. We say that you are an average of the five people you spend the most time with, including the ones inside of your head.

StarShine people look for ways to improve their own lives and they look for and acknowledge "WOWs" that other people produce. Kids at StarShine don't have to be told to pick up gum wrappers on the ground because they, themselves, don't want to see it. They pick up trash without being asked because they want to see beauty.

Creating WOW! unexpected, wonderful, off-the-charts, moment of experience, creates deep appreciation and a great memory. Positive customer and student experiences begins with the right promises, always under promise and over deliver. What are customer/student expectations in your family, school or organization? How does everything and everyone all fit together in order to make great experiences happen? Small, especially consistent things done really well can help to create that ultimate experience that causes people to say, "Wow." Here are some StarShine ideas and things we use:

- **Send your students or customers reminders by text, phone, or mail about school or business promotions**, sales, new products, and special events. Do something just a little differently even if it is just offering cheese and crackers, small promotional gifts, or a copy of a great student or teacher piece of art. Or have students make a piece of usable pottery that you give away in a drawing so people will come.
- **Have gift cards available for teachers, students, parents or customers**. They are an easy and convenient way to recognize efforts.
- **Have a loyalty club where students, teachers, parents,**

volunteers, vendors, and customers can earn points for rewards. Make it easy and don't have too many exceptions. Nothing ruins the "WOW" experience more than a long list of what "does not qualify" on a redemption loyalty card.

- **Remind families about important dates for testing or job fairs or other things they might have forgotten.** Be consistent, and show you are paying attention. It's a great way to stay in touch and say you care.

- **Have students and teachers create their own wish list and keep it on file.** Just think of all the significant others who would actually like to help and know what the person really wanted. By the way, our teachers make classroom requests on a great website for teachers' needs at http://www.DonorsChoose.org

- **Be a knowledge base for the community.** Know where the best vendors are, be willing to recommend them and exchange the list with everyone. Answer questions, know who or where to go to in case of an unknown contingency. Be that "go to" person and school. One time, one of the kids designed a placemat with the phone numbers and names of our favorite vendors. We decided to laminate it and mail five copies to each of our vendors with a note about how much we appreciate our favorite people. For years, people would call to get a placemat for someone new.

- **We hand out our "Sower" pins and other pins we buy and give away when others least expect it, to recognize someone's extra effort and "sowing hope and StarShine's message."** We have given these pins to a great waitress or people going out of their way to help us to have a great experience.

- **Hand out "Wow" cards that simply say, "You are important, you are making a difference in the world."** On the other side we have our website address. People love getting these. It is a small thing, but to acknowledge someone for doing special things is a big thing.

- **Teach employees to recognize and respond to everyone's**

attitudes and behaviors. Great experiences fly. The word will get out, and the people will come; students, parents, donors, volunteers, advocates and supporters. The other day, I observed a visiting gentleman asking one of our male students where to find the restroom. The boy did not point the way, he said, "Here let me take you there." I smiled, knowing that this boy would be a big success someday, as he has already developed the "StarShine WOW.

When people first meet me and find out about StarShine, one of their first questions is "What makes StarShine so different? What's the secret sauce? Why do you have to have all of K-12 inside of one school? Why do you teach all of this other stuff? Why teach gardening, art and music? Kids can't start businesses. Why do you have a radio station?" My first response is always, "It is the 'Whole' thing, not just a sum of parts." StarShine is an integration of many best practices about education and success in life. StarShine treats children as if each one has something so unique to offer, and it is our honor to seek out. We focus on the child's natural abilities to excel. We don't think all kids are at the same level just because they have reached a certain age. In fact, we rarely see two children of the same age, exactly at the same level of understanding or grade level.

We don't have the time to continue to lose student and teacher interest at the rate that we have been. We have been on a self-destructive path that needs to turn quickly. Life is not working for many, because we have gotten too far away from what makes it work or what makes us happy. We must make learning more relevant, significant and fascinating because we will all be learning at an exponential speed for the rest of our lives, as our lives continue to change at a never ending more rapid pace. Our very existence more than ever requires high-powered thinking and problem-solving, as well as high-powered knowledge that comes from learning and being able to use and quickly filter, facts. We must understand how to easily and rapidly enjoy and adapt to change and stay happy while we do. We must learn to collaborate, not only with technology but also in spite of it.

I think of the old Reader's Digest "Stress Tests" that used to tally a scorecard that would give a reader an indication of how much stress was too much. Things like losing a job, getting a divorce or moving all added up to "too much to handle." I can't imagine what today's scoring would be like. The potential stress that we all must endure at times seems nearly overwhelming…unless we are taught that it doesn't have to be hard. Coal turns into a diamond by just letting the pressure do its thing. Change can even be fun, or we can make it fun. Think about being on a Southwest Airlines' flight where the whole plane is laughing versus a plane ride with a rude flight attendant. We have all experienced that kind of "fear of flying" stress.

As we looked for successful school models, we learned a lot from Montessori and Waldorf Schools, and we continually were reminded of the "One-room schoolhouse" idea, where teachers were there to teach, to educe, to bring forward, the best of every single child in their multi-aged and ability classrooms. Teachers in one-room schoolhouses are typically without the resources of larger schools. Throughout history as well as today, multi-aged classrooms have shown greater individual student success than same-age classrooms. There are several factors that intertwine to cause this success. One primary factor is that the teachers who "choose" to work in a multi-aged classroom are usually more passionate and more motivated to make it work; they know it will take creativity and hard work. They are typically in underserved locations. They usually have had to work alone with all ages and few resources. But time and time again the children learn. The children coming out of multi-aged classrooms seem to learn to understand the value of the other students relative to their own significance and well being. Students in "one-room schoolhouses" are usually taught about nature because nature is usually right outside of the door. They are not in sterile classrooms that lack imagination, but rather in classrooms and situations that demand their imagination and their creativity. As the one-room schoolhouse children gain greater knowledge and manners, they usually progress to mentor the younger students, immediately impacting the whole group dynamics as individual needs are a part of the needs of the whole. They learn to become curious and to enjoy differences rather than only "tolerating" differences. Peer pressure and bullying is nearly non-existent, as a result. They get prepared for real-world experiences where everybody and everything is unique and being the same age as your co-worker is unusual.

7

AN UNINTENTIONAL LEAP OF FAITH

When you believe a thing, believe it all the way, implicitly and unquestionably...It's kind of fun to do the impossible.
-Walt Disney

I recently read *"Leap of Faith, Memoirs of an Unexpected Life"* by Queen Noor. I picked the book from my mother's bookshelf attracted by the title. My book, this book, *StarShine Effect*, could have easily had that same title, *"Leap of Faith, Memoirs of an Unexpected Life,"* as this is how I feel. The most unlikely, I would have consciously been the last picked to do this work. My friend, Annie Loyd Bachand introduces me often when I speak. She tells the story of being "pushed from a cliff and learning to fly" as she explains what happened to me.

I went to college at Fort Lewis College, in my hometown of Durango, Colorado wanting to learn everything I could about business and biology, especially the human brain, the human body and how to make the body "Olympic" healthy. I had aspirations of becoming a medical research scientist because I so revered the working human body and wanted to learn how to make it function at its peak. But after being disappointed in the medical field and its focus, not on health and well being, but rather on chemicals and strategies that alleviate symptoms, disillusioned, I gave up my medical career aspirations.

I was recruited to work for AT&T to become a part of a fast-paced young female executive program because they were trying to improve their Affirmative Action plan in hiring more female executives. I became immersed in the field of technology before most people knew what technology was.

I knew very little about being a corporate executive when I started that job but they were willing to develop my potential. They constantly tested us to further develop our "natural abilities." They gave us assessments that pointed out our weaknesses and our strengths. They constantly trained us and assessed us to see if we needed more help. I was fascinated with how they solved problems. Bell Labs was famous for their approach of allowing one group to think of wild ideas for change while another group tried to make the wild idea actually feasible. I forever will be appreciative of the time, expense and efforts that were spent on my behalf for training and development of my abilities at AT&T. Some of the tools that we teach StarShine students today are the direct results of that training I received while at AT&T.

Later, I was recruited away from AT&T, to work with the President of the Western Division for Mellon Bank in Denver, Colorado and for the next several years I was immersed in the international world of banking and real estate development. I learned a lot about managing (money) assets and also met a lot of insane people. They had a lot of money but no life. I wondered if money can't buy happiness, what is it for?

It seemed to me that money was an exchange of value. It is NOT the value. As the entire world, especially the United States, began to lose perspective of what real assets are, I began to lose more and more interest in being a part of the problem, banking. I ached at the way world priorities are established, and how a few people make decisions that have devastating effects on so many others.

For many years I have given speeches to groups of business people about various strategies and tactics for growing companies. But even years ago, I had become a voice for the need for K-12 education reform as I was worried about the level of education our children were getting, by what I was experiencing in hiring new employees. I witnessed a decline in quality resumes every year. As a business owner needing ethical, knowledgeable, balanced employees to work, I wasn't able to find them. As a mother of distinctively unique children, like other mothers' children, I was greatly disappointed in my children's school experiences.

I worked with many people, considered to be "successful" and was astounded at how many of the most talented have been the most miserable. For some reason it has seemed to me that the greater the individual's talents, the more others want to take it away. Today, too many adults are walking around as hurt children from whatever happened in the past. Real greatness is stopped short for people, as their true talents and abilities go ignored as they get busy with life in other directions. And everyone loses, because that one person's potential is gone from all of us. We are not taught how to look for and support the greatness in ourselves or in others. We have been told that we are not worthy of having great aspirations and ambitions, and that (total) success is for someone else. We are told that to be proud of our accomplishments is to feed our "bad" ego. We are taught to take care of everyone else before we take care of ourselves. Or we are told to be "Good to number 1" because no one else matters anyway, "You deserve it" we read in every magazine. "What happens in _____, stays in _____" as if we can hide from our own thoughts and feelings.

We have learned, taught and lived scarcity and fear...the exact opposite of what God teaches in almost any religion; we have taught this lack in our schools. Nature reflects the work of God in God's purest form, abundance. Why are we not teaching our children respect, discipline and that all things are possible, if you work at it?

There are only two things that really create or destroy us in the quality of life that we have, one is self-discipline and the other is meaningful relationships with others. Neither of those cost money, but they are not free. They become, over time the greatest assets that we own.

I have a picture of myself standing in front of one billion dollars in cash, brought to Phoenix by the federal treasury department. They had a road show to give people a chance to see it. Even though I had spent years in a banking career, I never saw that much cash. Money gives people so many choices. Maybe that's one reason that I enjoyed banking for so long, being able to witness the choices people made with their money. As my friend Dean Duperron says, "Without profit, there can be no philanthropy. Without revenue, you can't pay for what you want to do."

I love being around ideas and energy. My husband says that money is just green energy. But money is not an asset. The assets you acquire, or not, are determined by choices that you make; how you spend your money and time. Money buys things or creates liabilities depending on how you use it.

If I asked you what you would want if you could have anything, 80% of you would say "a million dollars." It isn't the money you want, it is what you can imagine doing with it, you want. Imagination is the key. Most people have no idea what they would do with a million dollars. Study after study has been done on people who win large amounts of money. Results continue to show that for most people, they are not happier after they have won money. Judging from the current economics of our United States, it would appear that many people have focused for too long on accumulating money and not on building a great life or a country full of assets.

Quite often I explain that StarShine is a kind of magic carpet that decides who will be on the ride and that included me. I did not foresee myself working in schools. This is true for many of the people that have joined in our efforts of creating the replicable StarShine Planet system and model for K-12 schools.

One of my friends, Paul Brinkley-Rogers, a former writer and Pulitzer Prize Winner for the Associated Press told me that he should write a book about the amazing people that have been attracted to StarShine and how being involved had changed their lives. He says that StarShine saves more adults than kids. Maybe someday he will write that book. In this one I try to describe what happened to a few of us.

8

MEETING WITH THE PRINCIPAL
THE MRS. SHOOP

"But friendship is precious, not only in the shade, but in the sunshine of life, and thanks to a benevolent arrangement the greater part of life is sunshine.
-Thomas Jefferson

It was 2003, and I was starting my second year at StarShine Academy and again I was turned down again for the charter I had applied for, so I was once again running my own "free" private school. The Charter approval board said what I was doing was too aggressive, would never work and they did not want me to waste state funds. So again, I went into my savings, the little I had left, and continued to fund StarShine. The charter board suggested that I get help in running my school to make things easier and perhaps another charter would "adopt" us and help us with finances. They referred me to another charter school and I met with their board and asked them for their help.

Another nightmare ensued. I had applied for our own 501(c)3 charity designation but it had not yet been approved. The other charter holder insisted that because she was adopting us, all monies had to go through her schools, even the donations that I brought in, which she took for her own operation. She was able to use our students as a part of her student income count, which provided more funding for her schools, but nearly zero for StarShine. By the time they went through all of their charges for helping us, most of the time all the money was spent, before we received any to run StarShine. This is not an unusual situation in our school systems.

We struggled with everything from not having enough curriculum to arguing over paying bills for items we needed and with the money I had raised. At times it seemed like I was the only one really looking out for the students' needs. I went to bed many nights wondering if I could keep things moving along and wondered why I ever decided to try to open a school. Many nights, I worried and I cried. I often told people how I never cried in my corporate American jobs but almost never stopped crying in my job inside of education. But there was one interesting introduction from this other school, Mrs. Shoop.

Mrs. Janis Shoop had been hired by the other charter to help all of their schools as one of their administrators and as a special education teacher. She had been a teacher in a large district and had been involved in some of the first charter schools in Arizona as an administrator. Her background in special education seemed impressive enough, as was her education history. I liked her, but I didn't trust her. I thought she was a spy from the other charter school, checking to see if I was giving them all of our money or not.

For months we were cordial but didn't talk too much. She worked with our special education students and went through our financial books. She seemed efficient and pleasant enough and the kids seemed to like her. But I still didn't trust her.

The students were learning and growing faster than we had anticipated, every day in every way. We had some ups and downs and real, terrible, tragedies, but, I was very proud of the students' growth and the school's work. The kids were learning and they were becoming inspiring to me and to one another. They seemed more engaged than ever in their own education and they were happy. We could hear it on the playground. There was a happy sound, not an aggressive sound like in many schools. The sound was so noticeable, many people commented about it. I was pleased, no matter what anyone else thought.

One Friday afternoon in April, Mrs. Shoop knocked on my door and asked to speak to me. "Oh great, now I get to talk to the Principal," I thought. Instantly my mind turned to wondering what I had done wrong. Isn't it funny how the word "Principal" seems to bring up a dreaded feeling that we have done something wrong, in most of us? Why is that? We called them "Headmasters" for a while to try to alleviate the fear, but everyone wanted to see the "Principal" so we changed it back.

Mrs. McCarty, she said, "I want to work here." I thought she was working there, so I said, "What do you mean?" thinking she might be suggesting that I leave. I was still in a funk. "I want to work directly for you, for StarShine, and not for the other charter anymore. I believe in what you are doing and I want to do it with you." I told her we didn't have any money and asked her what she wanted to do. "I will take your job as the Principal." A bit surprised, I was a little amused. "Well even if you came in as Principal, you wouldn't get paid, because there isn't any extra money. And I would still be here, making sure everything keeps running the way I believe it should, and I don't get paid either," I said. I will never forget what she said next, "It doesn't matter; we will figure it out together. This is an important project and we can do it better together." So the Principal, Mrs. Shoop was hired for no money for a month. Then I started to trust her.

Shortly afterward, Jan recruited her Mother, Lois Jamieson, to put our library together, read to the kids and form a group of girls along with Mrs. Jamieson's friends to teach a "Fashion Club" for StarShine. She brought the ideas back to her church, St. Barnabas Episcopal Church in Paradise Valley, and within weeks several of the groups there became a part of one or more departments at the school. Jan recruited her dad and some of his friends to build shelves for the school. It wasn't long before the church voted to make StarShine a "Lifetime Mission." All of this, started from Mrs. Shoop believing in the mission that drives StarShine.

It took us until the end of the second year to prepare any students to graduate, as none of the high school students could read past third grade reading when we first enrolled them. Each of the kids had to have one on one mentoring and we used every computer program we could find to help them learn easier. We used brain training techniques and speed reading courses. Each of the kids had transferred or dropped out of other schools in the district and had been told they would graduate in a year or so by those other schools, even with nearly straight F's on their records.

The number one reason for kids wanting to drop out of school is that they can't read. This fact made us vehemently focus on getting the kids to grade level in reading as fast as we could. Typical of StarShine, many miracles had to work together to be able to graduate any of them within two years, but we were able to get four ready. And we were proud of them.

Our first potential graduate was Janise and her story was not unique. I came to know Janise because I was the first person to speak with her when she arrived to enroll her daughter into kindergarten. I rarely enroll the students as we have a registrar in charge of student records and she also has a principal's certification, so she knows a lot more than I do about what information we need to get up front to be compliant. But for whatever reason, I was helping Janise to enroll her daughter and I noticed that she had outstanding handwriting. I asked her if she had graduated from a school in Phoenix. She admitted that she had dropped out of school because she had been pregnant with her daughter. Curious, since she was obviously bright, I asked her how close she had been to meeting graduation requirements. She told me she had no idea and that she had been cleaning houses during the past five years, barely making enough to take care of herself. I asked for her permission to obtain her high school records to see if we might help her to finish school.

The high school she had attended was about three miles from StarShine, so was fairly easy for us to receive Janise's school records. The Principal, Jan Shoop came running into my office when she got the file. "You won't believe this," she said, "Janise only had one-half of a credit to go for her to graduate and she had almost straight A's in school! Can you believe no one ever called her to let her know or persuade her to return to school, or even to let her finish on a homebound program?" I could believe it, as these kinds of "no one notices, no one cares" came up almost daily as we tried to help these kids. "It makes me so angry," I said, "that not only no one cared enough to try to help Janise, but that no one thought about the economic impact to society of letting someone so easily drop out of school. Do you think this country can survive this kind of irresponsibility?"

When we asked to have a meeting with Janise, she came to school apprehensively thinking something was wrong with her daughter. (This is another common problem, the only time anyone calls home from a school is when something is wrong, instead of something is right.) Janise came into my office along with Mrs. Shoop. I said, "Janise, you are going to become StarShine's first graduating senior, in the class of 2004." Janise looked at me with wide eyes and burst into tears, grabbing her face with her hands. "I can't believe it," she said, "I never thought this would be possible. I left that dream so long ago. I have been embarrassed for my daughter, because I never graduated. I can't believe it!"

As much as I wanted to bask in the happiness of the moment, I continued to feel anger toward this situation and the low level of where our society and education had plummeted to. Such a vast sea of non-caring. I vowed to find and help every young mother in similar circumstances to Janise.

We enrolled Janise into StarShine and helped to work around a schedule that would accommodate Janise and her family. That year, Janise brought four more of her friends to enroll at StarShine, all young mothers, all high school dropouts. She worked so hard every day and with so much enthusiasm and appreciation, she had a profound effect on the rest of the high school class.

Shortly after graduation, Janise continued her education and obtained a woman-owned certified business for her own corporation, establishing her own cleaning firm and employing five new workers. She began to pay taxes for the first time in her life. Janise bought a home in a beautiful area of northern Phoenix and got married.

If we only had that one story to tell about students at StarShine, I would say that I am pleased with our work, but in fact, that year, we had three more graduates having similar stories.

We had three girls and one boy graduate that year. They all had children of their own at the time. They all became extraordinarily successful. Maybe it was a coincidence that all of them ended up doing well with their lives or maybe it was a direct result of the inspiration, dedication and education that they received while briefly attending StarShine Academy. I choose to think the latter.

The boy graduated from college and became a technology administrator at a local technology company. One of the other girls graduated from cosmetology school and is working in her dream job, as a hair stylist. Another girl came up to me at graduation this past year and asked me if I remembered her. I see so many kids and I really did not recognize her. She explained that she was in our first graduating class and had gone on to college, graduated and now managed the retirement assets for a national investment firm. I would say four out of four doing well, is pretty extraordinary. And these four had been dropouts, typical of kids our society would have turned their back on…throwaway kids without stuff.

These kids all had some opportunity to get their GED certificate even though they dropped out of school but for whatever reason, they didn't. General Educational Development (or GED) tests are a group of five subject tests which, when passed, certify that the taker has American or Canadian high school-level academic skills. In questioning those kids and many hundreds more, I learned that they felt that achieving a GED did not feel as good as achieving a true high school diploma. There is a certain amount of pride that comes along with doing the work required to receive a full high school diploma and nearly every kid seems to agree about it. I have not met many students who were very motivated to receive a GED, although many have. On the other hand, I have met many previous drop-out parents who have explained to me how they wished they could return to high school and get a real high school diploma. It was a few months later that we decided to open the high school at night for any parents or community members to return to high school and receive a high school diploma from StarShine.

What happened at that 2004 graduation was not just for the graduates, though. I was proud of the school, the kids and parents. And I was proud to be a citizen of a country that supports innovation, even in education, through establishing the charter school concept so I could play a part. I wanted these families in this poor, urban neighborhood to be a part of this graduation in a big way.

I decided to hold the first graduation in the hundred-year-old Senate Building of Arizona's Capitol. When I first called to ask about scheduling the graduation, the woman I was talking to seemed to think I had lost my mind. "We don't allow graduations in our Capitol Building! These buildings are museums and still hold government policy meetings. There is no way you can come here for your graduation ceremonies." Obviously she did not know that I had made up my mind. "My children and families are all citizens of this state and of this country and yet none have ever felt empowered as such. I want them to experience the privilege of what it means to be an American and I want them to come to graduation ceremonies at our state's capitol. And besides, I am a taxpayer and have been paying for years for those buildings, and I would like to borrow them," I said. She continued to say, "No." But I asked her for other numbers and after a few days, someone decided that it wouldn't really hurt anything and she told me that we could hold our first StarShine graduation there.

Then I called the Superintendent of Public Education for Arizona, at that time, Tom Horne, (now Arizona's Attorney General) and asked if he would be our keynote speaker for the ceremony. He said he would. Then I called the "Toughest Sheriff in America," famous Sheriff, Joe Arapaio, who scared our kids and parents half-to-death most of the time, and asked him to also speak. I told him that it was a great opportunity to show his respect for underprivileged families trying to better themselves instead of always intimidating them. I told him it would look good in the press, besides. So he too, said he would come. Next, the best for last, I wanted to make sure I had everything lined up, I called my wonderful great friend and now StarShine Board Member, Vernon Parker, who at that time was the Assistant Secretary of U.S. Civil Rights. Vernon told his secretary in Washington, DC to rearrange his schedule for this prestigious event.

So the first StarShine graduation ceremony was accomplished with no less fanfare than the most revered of public events. Jan and I sat next to the kids. Rev. Joyce Bueker's played the harp and all of our board members came. The room overflowed with families and proud friends of the graduates, and the press who found out about Janise, decided to do a cover story for the Phoenix newspaper and put her on television along with her little girl.

We all had worked really hard that year, with a pretty tight budget, but we had accomplished great things. And we were proud of our work. We made a commitment to do even more. These kids, our future depended on it…America, in fact.

When we enroll students, we really get to know them. We don't just take in their name, address, emergency contact information and immunization. We use a detailed questionnaire list to get to know as much as possible about the students and their families. We want them to know we care about them as an individual, with specific needs, not as a number. We test them with fun assessments, mostly online, to determine what they really know and understand. And we get to know their likes and dislikes. We want to know about what they think of school and their families and what kinds of experiences they've had. We don't filter any out. We are there to find and grow human potential, not to eliminate it. We believe they each have successful opportunities if they can find them. We want to show them a path to find themselves. We say "We are helping kids to save themselves as fast as we can."

Jan and I worked together for nearly nine years, through many of Jan's health challenges, and probably spent more accumulative time together than with either of our husbands. I don't think we have ever said a cross word to each other. We have lived through many disasters but we help to hold each other's focus and attention on what we want, not what we don't want. We have tremendous faith, individually, and when we are together we demonstrate what the Bible says; "Where two or more are together…nothing is impossible." We know we are in a calling and will get whatever we need, when we need it, so we don't worry, much. We pray…we believe…we do it.

The work we are able to do internationally and daily has created a life that anyone would pay for, as we laugh, cry, feel everything and never know what exciting thing is going to happen next, or whom we get to meet. And every night I can close my eyes knowing that we have done our very best, that's all, and we are doing great work. And we get to talk together about the children's smiles. It's fun. It doesn't get much better than this.

We laugh about how much each of us has changed. Even our pictures from the beginning of StarShine to now are so different. We have grown right along with the kids and other adults, every single day. We share self-help books among hundreds of other books and we exchange "To Do" lists and our goals. We get excited about going to Staples, Costco and Home Depot together to buy supplies.

I share my concern for details, not micromanaging others, but micromanaging ourselves, individually. We use and teach how to use ABC lists, A for today's list, B for this week, and C to write things not to forget. We continually look for better personal, business or school processes and share what we have found. We both like to write so have written almost everything StarShine uses without much outside help. Until this year, Jan and I wrote nearly all of our grants because we were good at it and did not want the expense of an outside grant writer. (We probably should have hired outside grant writers a long time ago as it took a huge amount of energy and time for us to do this.)

We continually seek expert advice and go to as many seminars and conferences as possible to stay current with laws and best practices. This is probably our greatest leverage on our competition. I have seen and experienced this with other companies outside of education, as well. There is no greater way to know how to stay competitive than to attend seminars and talk to the people there. Jan and I attend conferences to learn from the speakers, but the true benefit of attending conferences is to be able to sit and talk to the people there.

Usually people attending conferences are already on the cutting edge, so the time spent for us, cuts through what might take months or even years to learn about. And with the global use of technology as an interface of human interaction, there is even a greater need to spend one on one, in-person time with others. Just one personal visit can expeditiously speed trust, partnership making and deal making, more than even ten years ago. It seems as though, with all of our technology, we are all starving for more personalized relationships.

Some of our best experts for StarShine processes came directly from meeting with a vendor or attendee of a conference we have attended. I have a friend who attends expensive conferences just so she can meet others who also spend thousands of dollars on conferences. She thinks they are the people she wants to do business with. Harvard has been using this strategy for years. There is no greater collaborating than what goes on between a group of Harvard graduates and their joint venture partnerships.

To learn more about managing yourself and your projects and to download free forms, take a look at the links in the Appendix of this book.

9

DESIGNING BEAUTY AND CREATIVE COMMUNITIES
ARCHITECTS DESIGN OUR FUTURE

""The longer I live the more beautiful life becomes. If you foolishly ignore beauty, you will soon find yourself without it. Your life will be impoverished. But if you invest in beauty, it will remain with you all the days of your life."
-Frank Lloyd Wright

Vernon Swaback was seventeen years old when he began to study as a protégé in 1957 to Frank Lloyd Wright, who at the time was one of the most famous, groundbreaking architects promoting organic and beautiful architecture. Frank Lloyd Wright wanted us to walk with nature rather than to stomp on it. Frank Lloyd Wright said his most profound mentor was established in kindergarten as his mother used the work of Friedrich Froebel "the children's garden" training using wooden cubes and colored balls for the child's imagination, "Gifts."

Vernon, even at his young age cared deeply about nature and the environment and how people could adapt to it, design within it, enjoy it and take care of it for future generations. For as long as he could remember, experiencing life as a philosopher and a dreamer added his own depth of perception to his creativity and talent. Vernon had great hopes for the way he might change the world under the tutelage of Mr. Wright. He could visualize a more congruent world, one that appreciates beautiful living and working spaces that harmonize with nature, rather than cause an infection.

But short were Vernon's vast experiences with Frank Lloyd Wright, which included Mr. Wright's death also in 1957. Heartbreakingly, he had to witness the huge electrical lines being constructed very near Taliesin West, obstructing Mr. Wright's view, and everyone else's of the beautiful Scottsdale, Arizona desert sky and mountains that he so dearly loved. These monstrous cables symbolized much of what was happening in the progressive times of the United

States' greed for growth, control and accumulation, with almost no regard for how it would devastatingly impact human life. Huge subdivisions were being formed of identical homes with no thought about how the people in them would actually live. The arts were becoming a superfluous addition to any development and to family life, and were struggling to find funding in the midst of the wealth that was being created and accumulated. Forests, farmland and beautiful old architecture was being destroyed at an alarming rate, causing people like Frank Lloyd Wright and Vernon Swaback to feel as if they were born in the wrong place at the wrong time.

Even as he was becoming one of the most sought-after architects in the world, Vernon continued to voice his opinions about how the world's people were destroying themselves because of their own stamping out of their own nature.

By the 1990's, Vernon began to lose almost all faith in societies' ability to change toward living in a more harmonious, robust way. Steeped in and surrounded by the most wealthy, privileged people on the planet, he was becoming increasingly disillusioned by the choices developers and private citizens were making about living in and building communities. Choosing to spend many hours in quiet contemplation, he became deeply saddened, sometimes even depressed about the mess we were in.

The day I met Vernon, our StarShine K-12 Academy had barely been formed, the playground was still bleak, the neighborhood trash still evident and the park across the street, still scary. Vernon was standing in the middle of the not so grassy, mostly dirt, play field with an attractive woman, one of his employees named Johanna, who accompanied him to StarShine.

He is a very tall, distinguished-looking man, always impeccably dressed, so as I glanced across the play area, he was impossible to miss. It is common for visitors to be on the campus, so it wasn't unusual to see someone new. "I wonder who that is." I said to myself. So I walked over to introduce myself. "Hi" I said, "I am Trish McCarty, Founder of this StarShine School, can I help you?" The woman spoke up, "This is

Vernon Swaback. He is a well-known architect, and we are talking about donating a mural to the school." Vernon interjected, "Frank Lloyd Wright talked about living as a creative community for forty years. I have been lecturing about it for thirty years and just wrote a book called *The Creative Community*. In two weeks, you opened one." He was standing close, in front of me. He is really tall. And as I looked up, into his kind eyes, I saw giant tears welling up.

Something happened on that day. Something shifted. I knew that Vernon would forever become an influence that I not only needed but craved. I would begin to ask his opinion about everything. Vernon would become a cornerstone of StarShine and all it stands for. He is a soul mate of mine in a profound sort of way and StarShine's. I had an instinctual feeling that everything that had ever been a part of my life was somehow intersecting to become something new on the day that I met Vernon. My friend, Patsy Lowry often reminds me that our life goes along until one day, and then you meet someone new that causes you to take a dramatic turn. Vernon caused my life to dramatically turn.

Vernon left the school that day, sobbing. We had both experienced *"The StarShine Effect"* which would become a description that many of us use when people visit StarShine and suddenly become immersed in a feeling that is almost indescribable. Many people start to cry. Most people can't leave; they feel compelled to become a part of StarShine in some way. We don't even try to explain it, we just describe what we can, "It's *the StarShine Effect*," we say. "It happens to most people. It moves your soul."

During the time Vernon spent talking to me on that day, he said something that I will never forget. We were discussing ideas of ancient philosophers and present day saviors. We were talking about the general state of leadership. He said architects are more important than religious leaders because they design how people are going to live together. When I asked him to tell me more, he showed many pictures to me of various communities in the world, including several that were developed around Arizona. He said that when builders began to build separate living areas with huge fences around houses and schools built on edge of towns, rather than in the center, society started to break down. He said that all people thrive on interaction with others and that when people begin to live separately, they begin to exhibit antisocial behavior. He said that today we have an enormous number of children who are raising themselves. They get up by themselves, hardly talking with anyone. They walk to school or ride the bus with earplugs in blasting music and they get to school where they are treated like numbers of cattle going through a gated system.

I couldn't help but remember my sharing a crazy honeymoon room with Dr. Leonora and how important that experience had been to me and to StarShine. I also thought about how absurd it seemed then, that I would spend time sharing a room with a stranger, but how fun and what a gift it had been. And I thought about all of the lonely kids out there.

It became obvious to me from that first interaction with Vernon, that what we were really developing at StarShine was a re-invention of what a great community village could be like; one that would inspire creativity, happiness and joy among its inhabitants, while developing a desire to live a responsible life. The question for me that lingered was how to put a "Creativity Community" inside or around an accredited K-12 little school design. I asked Vernon to join our board of directors.

Vernon wanted to make a substantial contribution to StarShine because he believed so much in its mission. So, he put much thought into what unique gift he could add, besides money, which he and his wife Cille, donated to us. He decided to design a mural in StarShine's honor and explained to me that he would give this mural as his statement explaining his view of StarShine.

Vernon Swaback has created his murals for his architectural work, famous throughout the world. His staff came along with him a few days later to tour the school and to explain the significance of the gift of the mural. His staff was very adamant when they mentioned how precious this gift was and how much it needed to be protected from the gang and tagging activity surrounding the school property.

I told Vernon that I was trying to create beauty for the neighborhood to try to reverse the energy from negative to positive. I explained to Vernon and his group that I had read with great interest about the "Broken Window Theory" in New York City, introduced in a 1982 article by social scientists James Q. Wilson and George L. Kelling who proved after years of research that when a window is broken in a neighborhood, crime increases within twenty-four hours. The reverse is also true; when a community beautifies a neighborhood and cleans up trash, the neighborhood begins to show signs of revival.

Vernon's group told me that they could not allow one of his large murals to become defaced by graffiti and that we needed to put the mural inside of a safe, protected area, hopefully, they said behind the bars surrounding the school. Adamant about my position, I turned to Vernon and said, "Vernon, I appreciate how famous you are and how precious and unusual your murals are, but you are alive and a human being and if something happens to it, you can come back over and fix it. I insist that we try this beautiful, museum quality, experiment for the neighbors to see and I truly believe that it will make a huge difference here." Vernon looked at me and with a giant smile, turned to his Swaback Partner team members and said, "Let's put it on the outside."

So the mural was painted to cover the entire wall next to the entry way to the school and is magnificent. We decided to put lighting on it in another faithful move so the neighbors could see it at night. We prayed too, that the lighting would be left alone. The week after the mural was finished, I had to drive past the school about nine o'clock at night to check on something. As I drove on to the street, toward approaching the school, I saw something that I shall never forget. In the dark, within the lighting against this amazing mural, stood five adults, quietly admiring this piece of heavenly beauty, a most unusual piece of artwork, given to this most needy place on earth.

Vernon wrote the following, fitting verse and forever placed it on a bronze plaque, permanently mounted at StarShine:

Garden of the Stars
Deep tones of the Earth
Along with colors symbolizing the atmospheric effects of the Arizona Sky
Flows together in a curvilinear geometry
Without beginning or end
The Star Shapes have been added by each of the Academy's Human Stars
The Garden of the Stars Mural
Is a reminder of
The bright and shining magnificence of what a single life can
Achieve when it is in harmony with the universal order
That is our shared and real home.
November 25, 2003
Designed by Vernon Swaback and
Executed by Swaback Partners

The mural has been there nearly ten years now and has never been touched by anything but love. The first graduating class, along with Vern's help, painted stars of their own on the top of the mural. They still bring people to see their "stars."

A few months later, another fateful event was to occur. Vernon brought his nephew, Bob Swaback to see us at the school. He was very kind and he spent quite a bit of time talking to the kids, which always impresses me a lot about adults. "Is it okay if I get some video players and televisions for StarShine?" Bob asked me. "Of course," I said. Well, Vernon had told him that I don't take donations from anyone who refuses to come and meet the kids, and unbeknownst to me, he was taking it seriously.

Bob came back a few days later, with a truck full of televisions, stands, cords and video players, along with videos to use, for *all* of the classrooms. And everything needed to be assembled so he brought tons of tools and asked the kids to help him. It was one of the most beautiful of days. The students took such great pride in helping him put everything together and were so excited about this new, fun equipment, they could hardly contain themselves. At the time very few of the kids had ever even seen a video recorder.

Bob seemed very proud of the kids, the school and his work that day. It was one of those most precious events that we get to experience as real blessings in our lives once in a while. Everyone could share in the love. But twists and turns happen in life that we are never prepared for.

It was only days later. Early one morning Vernon called me on my cell phone. His voice was shaking. "Trish, something has happened. I am not sure if it is Bob or his son. Someone has called me accidentally thinking that I am his father. There has been some accident and someone has drowned." As I listened to Vernon, I became weak. I think we all are shocked and have great empathy for any parent who loses a child, one of the most dreaded of fears. It was August 14, 2004, and it was Mitch, the only son of Bob and his wife, Gaye and Vernon and Cille's grandnephew. He was twenty-three years old.

When I got to the school a couple of days later, I went in to the high school and told the kids about the accident. Some of the kids cried as they recounted stories that Bob had told them about his son. I left the high school class and went back to my office with a heavy heart. I was sitting at my desk, feeling so sad when some of kids knocked on my door a few hours later. I was overwhelmed as I was presented with touching cards and letters from every student and every teacher at StarShine to forward to the Swaback family. The kids, without me asking, had decided to give something they could, back to someone so generous to them.

We received a card from the Swabacks describing the importance of receiving the letters with a picture of the Swaback family sitting in the midst of the mounds of cards. I keep that picture to remind me of small and large acts of kindness; they always return, maybe not the way we expected, but generosity and love always returns.

10

CHAORDIC DESIGN AND THE FIBONACCI SERIES: CREATIVITY IS BORN FROM STRUCTURE

I MET JACK RING; ONE OF THE FIVE SMARTEST BRAINS ON THE PLANET

"The new American Dream, though, the one that markets around the world are embracing as fast as they can, is this: Be remarkable, Be generous, Create art, Make judgment calls, Connect people and ideas…and we have no choice but to reward you." –Seth Godin

Jack Ring was born on black Friday in the middle of Kansas, in the same room his father had been born in, on the day of the worst dust storm ever to hit Kansas. They had to put blankets up around the walls to protect baby Jack from breathing in dust. He was a brilliant child. His parents paid attention to his ideas and helped him to use his brain to its fullest capacity. StarShine became a beneficiary of those parents' offspring that will benefit all kids, all over the world, forever.

To form the foundational, organic, strategic design of the school, we implemented a systems management idea that was mentioned many times by Dee Hock, the former President of Visa, called "Chaordic." It is a blend of chaos and order, and represents growth and structural design according to nature, like a spider web, a brain or the Internet. Visa used this design to build a company valued at over several billion dollars in just two years starting with only thirty-five people. In Hock's book, *One from Many: VISA and the Rise of the Chaordic Organization,* he made several predictions about the future design and operation of communities. In 1998 at an annual conference Dee Hock explained the following predictions that we are now living today:

"More than thirty years ago, I became obsessed with three questions which have since dominated my life. They were relevant then. They are compelling today. They are the heart of our subject this morning.

Why are organizations, everywhere, whether political, commercial or social, increasingly unable to manage their affairs?

Why are individuals, everywhere, increasingly in conflict with and alienated from the organizations of which they are part?

Why are society and the biosphere increasingly in disarray?

Today, it's apparent to anyone who cares to think about it that we are in the midst of a global epidemic of institutional failure. Not just failure in the sense of collapse, such as the Soviet Union or corporate bankruptcy, but the more common and pernicious form -- institutions increasingly unable to achieve the purpose for which they were created, yet continuing to expand as they devour resources, demean the human spirit and destroy the environment:

> Schools that can't teach,
> Corporations that can't cooperate or compete,
> Unhealthy health-care systems,
> Communities without communication,
> Welfare systems where few fare well,
> Police that can't enforce the law,
> Judicial systems without justice,
> Governments that can't govern, and
> Economies that can't economize.

Four centuries ago, Machiavelli wrote:

"As the doctors say of a wasting disease, to start with, it is easy to cure but difficult to diagnose. After a time, unless it has been diagnosed and treated at the outset, it becomes easy to diagnose but difficult to cure. So it is in government. We are at that very point in time when a 400-year-old age is dying and another is struggling to be born - a shifting of culture, science, society, and institutions enormously greater than the world has ever experienced," he said. *Ahead, the possibility of the regeneration of*

individuality, liberty, community, and ethics such as the world has never known, and a harmony with nature, with one another, and with the divine intelligence such as the world has never dreamed."

He and those like him, including our own Jack Ring, are always far ahead of time and advanced in their thinking. They have made and continue to provide a significant impact on those of us in corporate America looking for a new, more harmonious, more profitable, less-stressful way of achieving "breakthrough" business. Being in banking myself, I was compelled with this idea of working with inspired people rather than "controlled" people.

Visa has now changed from the original structure and not so "chaordic" anymore. But the work that Dee Hock and others did to show us the way has impacted the way all organizations, corporations and families must think.

Having been in banking and reading about, while witnessing the surge of Visa, I had come across many manuscripts written by a person named Jack Ring, a strategic systems engineer and mathematician. His work fascinated me, as I had always been interested in Quantum mechanics and futuristic systems design. When the Internet and Google made it easier to get my hands on high quality White Papers, I couldn't get enough of reading the writings of Jack Ring.

I decided to try to find and recruit him. It wasn't easy, even using Google, LinkedIn, and others to find Jack Ring's contact information, but I finally found a telephone number that was at the bottom of one of the white papers he had written titled "Designing the Best Solution, Not the Best Guess." When I dialed his number, the phone rang and was picked up by an answering machine with a lady's voice saying, "You've almost reached Jack Ring. Please leave a message." I was so excited that I had nearly connected with a man who many believe is one of the top five smartest brains on the planet, alive today. I spoke quickly as I left my message, saying something like; "Mr. Ring, I know how busy you are and many people want to talk to you, but I think we have started a Chaordic solution to K-12 education that could change the world of education, if I don't mess it up. I promise not to waste your time, but I think you might really want to know about this. And I could really use your help."

About five minutes went by when my phone rang. "This is Jack Ring" the slow talking, low-voiced man said. I could hardly believe it. I was so excited; I started talking immediately to give him a quick description of what we were up to and how important it would be. I asked if he would look at what we had put in place to see if it might be a true "Chaordic" business strategy that would work, a K-12 education solution that could grow organically and quickly rather than one that would be designed and controlled by one person as a CEO. I asked him if I could meet with him for only one-half an hour. I did not know where he was and for whatever reason, I thought he might be in New York City, but I didn't care as long as I could meet him.

His answer was part of the "StarShine Effect." He said "Well, not before 2:30." Stumped and not wanting to say anything that might delay his enthusiasm, I said, "Perfect, um, where are you?" He paused for a couple of my excruciating moments and then with a little chuckle he said "Scottsdale."

This chuckling that Jack exhibits from time to time has endeared him to me; besides that fact that I do believe he is the smartest man on earth. He has been able to maintain a child-like quality of laughter and simple joy in being cleaver and mischievous at times as he gets people to look inside of their own beliefs and expertise. I have watched him brilliantly put people in their place with a few of his precise words.

From the Internet to handling security, we have a "Whole" new world. And we don't know how to "do" it. We have had no preparation for the kind of change and the changes that we are now living. We are constantly connected to so much information and movement. Everything is everything. We really can't make small chunks make sense. We are immersed in a world where we can experienced the ripple effect almost immediately because communication is so automatic. In years past, none of us had to experience the pain being experienced of someone halfway around the world. But today people are putting pictures and descriptions of tragedies in our face almost instantaneously. We aren't able to ignore sadness or inhumane action like we used to be able to. We have daily experience that proves now that we are really, truly connected to one another. But we have not had the training to deal with it. We don't really know how to live in a world that is so confusing, complicated and connected. We have not been taught how to be or stay happy and productive in spite of change. Most of us have not been taught how to enjoy change. We somehow keep thinking that we have an ability to create structure and permanence or that we can predict our own future.

A great example of "Chaordic growth" is Alcoholics Anonymous. It has incorporated great advice for those afflicted with alcoholism and their families, but everyone's life could be improved by memorizing a few lessons taught by this wonderful organization. One of their often-used prayers is the Serenity Prayer:

> *"Lord, make me an instrument of your peace. Help me to accept the things I cannot change and to change the things I can. And Lord, give me the ability to know the difference."*

I was asked by Jack Ring, "What would I be willing to die for?" I said that I was not in this work to die for anything before I actually *have to*. He kept asking me the question until I thought, "Well if someone tried to break into the school and hurt one of the children, I would do anything to protect them." It is what he wanted to hear, I guess, because from then on, he has been one of my most attentive advisors.

Jack knows a lot. He has worked on strategic designs for so many companies, he can't even name them all and he is an amazing mathematician. It was Jack that led us to discover the perfect number of students for a school to operate at maximum efficiency in human behavior and financial management, four hundred, partly predicted by the perfect number of full-time adults working together; no more than twenty.

The first several years we only had about one hundred students in our schools because of the limited space. I personally was glad with having smaller schools, as I wanted to manage fewer kids because I needed to be able to watch reactions to the school design and record them. With fewer kids, the data collection was easier. Financially, though, it was constantly difficult to purchase all that we needed for thirteen grades with the income from only one hundred students.

As Jack continued to work with us for "free" to monitor our ability to create a "Chaordic Design" he began talking to us about another fascinating and seemingly related subject: the Fibonacci series. The Fibonacci series or sequence, featured in the Tom Hanks, 2006 movie, *The Da Vinci Code,* is a mathematical series of numbers described and realized by Leonardo of Pisa (1170-1250), nickname Fibonacci, whom was born in Pisa, Italy. He made many contributions to mathematics, but is best known by laypersons for the sequence of numbers that carries his name:

0, 1, 1, 2, 3, 5, 8, 13, 21, 34, 55, 89, 144, 233, 377, 610, 987, 1597,

This sequence is constructed by choosing the first two numbers (the "seeds" of the sequence) then assigning the rest by the rule that each number be the sum of the two preceding numbers. This simple rule generates a sequence of numbers having many surprising properties. Here are a few:

- Take any three adjacent numbers in the sequence, square the middle number; multiply the first and third numbers. The difference between these two results is always 1.
- Take any four adjacent numbers in the sequence. Multiply the outside ones. Multiply the inside ones. The first product will be either one more or one less than the second.
- The sum of any ten adjacent numbers equals 11 times the seventh one of the ten.

Fractals are another phenomenon of math and nature explaining a repetitious design, having something to do with "chaordic growth." According to *Wikipedia,* "There are several examples of fractals, which are defined as portraying exact self-similarity, quasi self-similarity, or statistical self-similarity. While fractals are a mathematical construct, they are found in nature, which has led to their inclusion in artwork. A fractal is "a rough or fragmented geometric shape that can be split into parts, each of which is (at least approximately) a reduced-size copy of the whole, a property called self-similarity. Roots of the idea of fractals go back to the 17th century, while mathematically rigorous treatment of fractals can be traced back to functions studied by Karl Weierstrass, Georg Cantor and Felix Hausdorff a century later in studying functions that were continuous but not differentiable."

The term "chaordic" according to Dee Hock and others is

1. Any self-organizing, self-governing, adaptive, nonlinear, complex organism, organization, community, or system; whether physical, biological, or social, the behavior of which harmoniously blends characteristics of both chaos and order.

2. An entity whose behavior exhibits observable patterns and probabilities not governed or explained by the rules that govern or explain its constituent parts.

3. Characteristic of the fundamental organizing principles of evolution and nature.

Jack was spending enormous amounts of time and energy (with and to teach me) and I began to feel as if we really were onto something very, very big. We watched as Twitter and Facebook began to have tremendous seemingly "organic" growth out of great designs. I kept encouraging Jack to make sure to the best of his ability that I did not put any practices into the system that would stifle the ultimate "chaordic" growth of StarShine Academy Schools.

Harland Cleveland discusses the opposite of a centralized organization (a hierarchical organization with a central control or boss). He says that the opposite is not decentralized with leadership on the outskirts, but an uncentralized leadership in which communication flows from point to point, groups form for one purpose, disband, then another group forms somewhere else around some other purpose. You can envision this as the difference between a pyramid and a spider's web. The extreme example of the centralized government is the military. A decentralized organization is one that keeps dividing and subdividing into different areas and departments that are still linked by one central leadership. A good example of the uncentralized system is the Internet with no one having direct control and many points of information in which individuals come together for various purposes and then disband when the purpose is complete or the individuals have met their needs.

For the chaordic process to really take hold, to really work, to really grow, each of us needs to consider how we are part of this. What voice do we want to have in where our organization goes in the future? This can only happen if leaders take an active role. We can each have the opportunity to decide for ourselves how we wish to be affected and then make that happen. In an uncentralized organization, each of us can be in communication with others all over the world, creating a web or net of support for each other, and making changes that will help us better to meet the needs of the mission and one another.

I am convinced that chaordic is the only way to build a business today, having the ability to change and grow with the requirements of today's world; the trick in the beginning of StarShine was to be able to define and refine the "DNA" of the best of best school processes, so that once implemented it would become a self-sustaining, self actualizing, constantly improving system. Jack Ring, has been able to guide many of the outcomes of StarShine by continually helping to remind me to stay out of my own way and to allow the process to work.

We devised a plan to set up a separate "for profit" organization, similar to a combination of a trusted friend, co-op, consultant and franchise, StarShine Planet, which would help to continually grow, help to fund and nurture StarShine Academy Schools, and to maintain tools to develop balance in the mind, body, spirit, health, wealth and happiness within the teachers and children. Our vision to create 1,000 campuses that would graduate 30,000 students annually with a Bachelor-degree equivalent level of knowledge prior to the age of 18 helped to develop our model. StarShine Planet would begin to provide the center of expertise and systems that would support the co-op network of schools and what they need to do their jobs. It would research and create safe, fun environments for meaningful learning and encouragement to "educe" the very best of each child. We would research and establish ways to help to prepare teachers and students for the wonderful world that they will help to grow, produce and live in. And we would do it as fast as possible. We would help kids to save themselves as fast as we can.

Jack Ring is part of the Futures' Society and several years ago, invited me to one of their meetings at a local technology college to listen to his presentation about the importance of StarShine's growth to change the way we look at K-12 education. I sat across the table from a friend of Jack's, Dr. Byron Davies, who kept explaining words to me that I had never heard. Dr. Davies is another super smart human being having Ph.D.'s and undergraduate degrees from Stanford, CalTech and MIT in engineering, so he could give me clues to the theories and substantiated studies that Jack kept referring to.

This meeting of Dr. Davies was again another example of StarShine's synchronicity at work, as Byron and I became good friends and he eventually came to work for us. StarShine began to be an obsession for him as well, as the more research he uncovered, the more excited he became about what StarShine represented. Dr. Davies had graduated college by the time he was eighteen and had many sad stories about how he felt when he was a real "geek" in school. Both of his children, and his wife, are equally brilliant and had tons of stories about what they felt was wrong with our education system. It was during these many visits with Byron that I realized "high-risk" students and underprivileged kids might be from any family and not just poor ones. In working with Byron, I began to believe that our children in every school were potentially "at risk of failure" not necessarily because of the child's family's background but because of how our education system had developed to ignore their unique needs.

Dr. Davies began to guide all of our technology and business infrastructure and the main liaison to Jack Ring and their circle of world- class scientist friends. We eventually developed a Genius Roundtable Council of Expert Advisors who all have stunning credentials. They meet and discuss current theories and compare them with findings from scientists and philosophers from long ago and how we might include it in StarShine.

I am a hobbyist of analyzing information, perhaps much lighter than Byron, Jack or our Genius Roundtable, but it is certainly stimulating and fascinating to learn of their conclusions and how we might integrate complex theory to create a simplified system that others can use and evolve. Jack says that it is easy to make things complicated, like our current education system, but it takes shear brilliance to make complicated systems easy to use. Google search engines are a perfect example and that is one of our visions: to make StarShine and K-12 learning so easy and so fun that no student will resist it. We see learning as something that kids can't wait to do, like the way kids used to get up early on Saturday morning to watch the really sweet, simple and funny cartoons on television like they had in the old days.

Learning tools and brain research continues to escalate as everything else on the Internet every day and Byron keeps us informed. Byron was the main reason we were able to solidify a strong relationship and partnership with Arizona State University Skysong Innovation Center, one of the smartest moves we made, by taking an office there. He keeps us tied in to Stanford and the innovation going on there in brain and education research.

He shares the passion with everyone at StarShine about saving kids. I usually get up around 4:30a.m. in the morning and I go to bed around 9:30p.m. Byron sometimes goes to bed AFTER 4:30a.m. so we get a kick out of sharing several Google links in the middle of the night, and sometimes jokes. Byron and I follow fairly serious Yoga paths of exercise and practice, so we have a lot in common. Like everyone else at StarShine, we are developing lifetime friendships as we learn how to work for StarShine's future.

Jack, Byron and I believe that work is not a forty or fifty hour workweek but should be a lifetime passion. It just is what we do and it might be any time or any day, but is far from being the vision of the 1980's workaholic of Tom Cruise's version of "The Firm." We believe if the world becomes sustainable for future generations it will be because people want to do it, as sustainability of anything is seventy-five percent behavioral. Including how we learn and how we teach.

TRISH MCCARTY

11

BRANDING STARSHINE

SCOTT LERMAN: FOR LOVE NOT MONEY

"Not what we have but what we enjoy constitutes our abundance."
-John Petit-Senn

Imagine if you could grow the world's best schools where they've never grown before, sow them like seeds through the countryside, into the cities, and across the planet. At StarShine Academy, that's not just our dream, it's our mission.

Scott Lerman, President of Lucid Brands and one of the top branding professionals in the world wrote our poignant mission statement. He also created our logo, a Johnny Appleseed figure of a Sower, depicting our students throwing stars of hope out into the world, walking on a solid path: STARSHINE ACADEMY.

In 2004, a group of MBA graduate students from Thunderbird International University of Global Management, considered by U.S. News and World Reports Magazine in ranking colleges, to be the number one international university for CEOs, lead by Jason Passe, Michelle Gansle, Laura Scherer, Ramesh Srinivasanand, Matt Dixon and Greg Whelan, came to meet with me in my office at StarShine to discuss their proposition. As a part of their final exam, they wanted to work on StarShine's business plan, enter a regional contest for marketing and perhaps compete in an international contest in New York City at the American Marketing Association's International Offices. I looked at these obviously brilliant young professionals with surprise. "I don't know if you guys have noticed, but this is not big business, we are a small school in a tough neighborhood full of kids that few people want or care about. Don't you usually work with large companies like Dupont and American Express?" Undaunted, they were excited and prepared to support their ideas. They told me that what we

119

were doing could bring about world peace and greater financial stability and what we were trying to do is so important; they had to go for it. I told them that if they wanted to do it, they were not going to get much help from me as I was just too busy running the school.

The team won the regional competition and was invited to compete in the national contest. They asked if some of us could accompany them to New York City to watch them compete against tougher competition at the American Marketing Association Offices in Time Square.

I watched them as they walked onto the stage in their StarShine shirts, wearing their StarShine lanyards with their pictures, names, ambassadorships and goals. They reached their hands out to each of the judges to shake hands and introduce themselves in the "StarShine Welcome" format, known and practiced by all StarShine kids, starting in kindergarten.

Not only did their business and marketing plan win, it won by a landslide, with all eight of the judges' unanimous vote. The plan was written like most business plans but included pictures of the kids and a vision for replicating "Peace Teaching." They developed our idea of a franchise-co-op and a timeline for growth. They believed the pent-up demand was extraordinary and nothing anyone has ever experienced.

They walked out on the stage and blew the judges away as they acted like StarShine kids when they shook the judges' hands. They showed the business plan as a PowerPoint. Their excitement was infectious. The income projections seemed ridiculous but believable.

The judges were a who's-who panel of top business and marketing people, among them, Scott Lerman, of Lucid Brands, who had been responsible in-part for the famous branding that revived Harley Davidson, 3M, American Express and Caterpillar.

Scott Lerman approached me after the meeting and said that he wanted to work with me. I repeated what I had told the Thunderbird students; we were small and could not afford someone of his stature, and perhaps it was overkill, anyway. I said, "Scott, I can't even afford this discussion. I have to concentrate on getting the kids shoes, not branding." He had planned an upcoming trip to visit Phoenix with Thunderbird in the next week and suggested that he come by to see the school and talk to some of our constituents.

When he arrived at the school, he wanted to talk to students, parents, teachers, the board and some volunteers. He spent the next three days at StarShine trying to learn everything he could from whoever would talk with him. He took pictures and videos and seemed to be all over the place. I was getting nervous watching him. He was powerful and opinionated and I wasn't totally sure about his motivation.

Toward the end of his visit, he asked to speak to Jan and me. He told us that what we had accomplished was something that everyone wanted but nobody had. He said there was a world pent-up market for what we had done in K-12 education, and demanded, "I am not going to be left off of this ship." He said he had rarely been inside of a company where everyone agreed and was focused on the mission. He explained further that when we finished putting everything together, the landslide of attention we would get would be greater than any he could imagine.

Scott immediately began helping us for love, not money. The weekend that he returned to New York City, he created, and is the spokesperson on a video that we put on the front of our website and is still one of the best videos produced explaining what StarShine is. He developed our mission statement, brochures, our logos and our colors. He looked at what we had previously produced and used what he could by repackaging and redesigning it.

Our original logo had a child reaching for the stars and a tagline that I made up with some help from others that said, "Every child is a SuperStar." Scott explained that people supporting the mission don't want to be supporting kids getting ready to be superstars. He said it was too confusing. I admitted that some people thought we were growing theater talent or the next NBA players. He said the kids aren't reaching for the stars, they are throwing stars of hope out to everyone else and giving everyone help once they are in StarShine.

There are thirteen stars to depict the thirteen grades: K-12, and the child is a Johnny Appleseed type of sower we call "Sowie" walking on a strong path of STARSHINE. The tagline Scott made up is more appropriate, "Realizing Dreams Through Education." I still sign my name with "Together Growing Tomorrow's SuperStars" because I still believe that in each of us is a "SuperStar" at something and we all need to help one another bring that superstar quality out so that the world will benefit.

A few months before Scott was introduced to us, we were given a barn-raising effort by Valley Partnership, a real estate and builders' community organization. Over 500 charities, companies and individuals came together on one Saturday morning and renovated the entire property. One of the Valley Partnership member companies had designed a sign and helped redesign our original logo, which I had originally designed myself. The group donated one-half of a million dollars worth of in-kind and free materials toward what we called a "barn-raising." Scott took hours to study the information they put together and used many of those ideas to improve upon.

Scott brought together some of his previous work with his colleagues from New York to make what Valley Partnership had given us, even better. I have worked with many branding and marketing people during my career with large companies but have never worked with anyone as talented as Scott in branding and marketing. He is amazingly creative and quick. He can listen to a few people and immediately understand how to design an idea, a logo or a video that tells a whole story about a company toward creating a solid culture, the most important part of any group. That is what branding and marketing people are supposed to do, but too many just aren't all that effective. Through the right message an entire company can develop precise methods and a culture driven by following their mission. It is amazing how important branding is to a company's success and how both large and small companies ignore or make huge mistakes in this endeavor.

I now have known and worked with Scott and his people for

several years and I truly enjoy watching his creative processes, springing out of structure. Several times Jan and I have traveled to New York and Scott has been generous with his schedule to spend time with us to update whatever we need to. He is another example of incredible people involved in the "calling" of StarShine. Had it not been for Scott, we probably would not be called the "Johnny Appleseeds of Education."

Scott has never asked for anything; not money or promises. He has put his heart into helping StarShine because he believes in the mission of helping every child and he believes that StarShine has the ability to make it a reality. He wants to be a part of it. He told us that StarShine has developed a brand that stands for integrity, purpose and mission and it will easily become a trusted brand of approval for anything for children, almost like the old "Good Housekeeping Seal of Approval." StarShine has become the voice of trust for parents of K-12-aged children, even for clothes and toys.

It seems we hear of fewer companies lately having established enviable reputations by creating profits from purpose, as in one of my favorite books by Ian Percy, "The Profitable Power of Purpose." Corporate, social and business leaders are too often discovered to be involved in scandals and cover-ups. Once revered church leaders, politicians and bankers have abused the public's trust. The general public questions marketing campaigns because the truth is often obscured by fancy ads and quotations. The Internet can be manipulated to give messages that aren't true. Reputations have been made and ruined by effective Internet strategies, whether or not they are based on facts or fiction.

Hopefully, leaders of companies, countries, churches and families will realize soon, that their own happiness depends on each choice they make and how they choose to live and give; not as much on how much money they accumulate, but on how much good they do. Perhaps with the exposure of information easily accessed by the Internet and other communication, people might start to turn toward a more just life where they desire to make more humane choices that create more sustainable outcomes for true abundance and happiness.

There are several attempts currently to create for-profit, tax-paying companies combined with the drive, passion and responsibility that usually define the non-profit world. One movement, to create a "B" Corporation has had success in several states for legislative approval. It is a "for" profit, taxpaying, corporation but is driven by social responsibility. "C" Corporations, by law, must derive the greatest return to its investors, no matter what it does to the public good. All of us can think of some large companies whom have acted irresponsibly and caused tremendous environmental or social damage, in their pursuit of financial and investment gains. Public scrutiny and easier access to information has begun to put pressure on corporations to behave. But a new wave of responsible C Corporations have adopted by-laws that explain their mission toward public good, even when a decision might hurt investors. Whole Foods, is one such company. They are one of the largest publically traded companies with specific practices to uphold their mission of providing the best and healthiest food and has been ranked as the most socially responsible. Individuals and special interest groups hoping to obscure their wonderful public image constantly attack them.

A trend in venture capital and investment groups toward investing in "Triple Bottom-Line Companies," (good for the planet, good for the people and good for profit) seems to also be predicting a change in the way we will do business in the future, I hope. Our strategic partners, touchPoint Partners out of Boulder, Colorado demand corporate responsibility. Their mission is:

> *At touchPoint Partners, we define Corporate Social Responsibility as the way in which a company directs its profits to improve social, environmental and economic circumstances in our world. We examine our partners' current strategies and determine how to better align their activities to meet their goals.*

I don't believe anyone can replicate a school any more than a teacher, student, family or community. Schools are a complex system of humans, all with different fingerprints. But I sincerely believe that schools can leverage one another to share what works, marketing, branding, buying power, legal power and opportunities to share with teachers and students, like field trips and EcoTravel. StarShine schools are usually non-profit, or we recommend that they organize and are managed "by and for" their local community. But as a corporation wanting to expand our support of large networks of schools, we felt that it would be irresponsible to investors and to the public not to pay taxes. After studying Whole Foods and "B" Corporation recommendations, and working with international companies, we decided to form StarShine Planet as a blended franchise/co-op socially responsible model "C" Corporation adopting bylaws and practices aligned to "B" Corporations. By setting our company up as a one-stop resource center, each school would be able to obtain bulk pricing, lower direct costs and benefits, while sharing best practices and expertise, as well as marketing. Luckily, as we were designing and building StarShine, the public was changing to demand greater transparency and social responsibility for all businesses.

Schools and districts have historically wasted millions of dollars with too much bureaucracy, too many layers and too many places to lose money. StarShine believes small schools, managed correctly, sharing with many other small schools, making local decisions and leveraging marketing dollars is the most efficient and effective way to deliver the best education.

In 2010, we joined Arizona State University Skysong Innovation Center opening its doors as an incubation-accelerator center, helping companies to grow by bridging businesses with the university to effect global change. At Skysong there is a focus on green, high tech companies as well as those like StarShine, focused on working toward peace through innovation, strategy and economic development. Several of the companies located there are mission-driven "to do well by doing good."

12

PARTNERING WITH A ROCK STAR
MEETING PRINCE CHARMING

Don't hate me because I'm fabulous.
-Prince

This chapter was one I was not going to include. But after being told by Mom that I had to because it is so much a part of StarShine, this story like everything else in StarShine, ensued.

Now 2005, three years into StarShine and sixty years after 1945, World War II, and the devastating nuclear bombs dropped on Hiroshima and Nagasaki, Japan, ending the war. Zen Buddhist Monks from Japan had started a flame from the burning embers of Nagasaki and Hiroshima and had kept the flame alive for sixty years, praying for peace every day. Peace groups from around the world were working with the monks to return the flame to its place of origin, where the first atomic device was detonated, on the White Sands Missile Range at the Trinity Test Site in Trinity, New Mexico. According to Zen tradition, the sixty-year cycle was ending and the flame needed to be returned to symbolize a new peaceful beginning. The monks would travel 1600 miles from San Francisco, mostly by foot, carrying the lantern with the flame, to bring it back, to extinguish it on August 9 in a ceremony at its birthplace. The first bomb was dropped on Hiroshima, Japan on August 6, 1945 and the second at Nagasaki on August 9, 1945. The closing ceremony would include about one hundred people from around the world, praying together that nuclear weapons never again be used.

Matt Taylor had contacted me and others involved at StarShine to ask if we would help to host the monks at StarShine Academy as they walked through Phoenix on July 28th and 29th because of our efforts in teaching peace. Matt grew up in Japan, was bi-lingual and helping to organize the complicated events for the monks along with negotiating with the United States military to allow access to the military site in

New Mexico. He and Martin Sheen were filming —Atomic Flame, Three Minutes to Midnight as a documentary of the current walk and its history, and asked if some of us would meet the walkers as they arrived and continued the walk through Phoenix. He asked if we could host the monks at the school with a community luncheon. He also asked us to meet them in Albuquerque to travel to the site with them and participate in the solemn ceremony at Trinity with other invited guests.

This, like much that happens at StarShine was so synergistic and meaningful to me, having spent so much time in Japan; Matt had no idea about my own experiences. So of course I was honored beyond explanation, to be able to participate in this significant event. Terri Mansfield, my friend and Peace Department activist coordinated with the Franciscan Renewal Center in Paradise Valley, close to Phoenix, to allow rooms and dinner for the night for the monks and film crew.

Several of us met the monks as they entered downtown Phoenix and walked with them seven miles toward a meeting at the mayor's office. This was on July 28, 2005 in Phoenix, Arizona. Anyone having visited Phoenix knows about the intense heat and sun that blazes Phoenix summer days and this was no different. I was boiling hot, in my white T-shirt, pouring water on my head to try to keep cool. I had to continually remind myself that I had to keep going to be able to keep walking. Each time I thought I might faint, I looked over to watch these cheerful black-robed monks, one in his late seventies, walking as if it was no big deal, mumbling semi-silent prayers and meditations, the entire distance. It was remarkable!

After the mayor's meeting we had a beautiful (hot) luncheon at the school where many guests came to participate and meet the monks. We stood by the Peace Pole in the garden and took hundreds of pictures. That evening a few of us traveled (by car) to meet the monks at the Franciscan Renewal Center for dinner. When we arrived, we had to laugh. The monks had created clotheslines with string from religious cross to cross at the Catholic retreat so they could hang their robes to dry after hand-washing them. After dinner, we agreed to meet them at

5:00 a.m. the following morning to walk with them as they began their journey toward New Mexico. I was exhausted and every part of my body ached from the seven mile heated walk the day before, but I couldn't refuse this request from these sweet, devoted people. So my friend Maren Showkeir and I met Terri Mansfield and the crew at the Franciscan Renewal Center a few minutes before 5:00 a.m. to walk with them again. This time, my feet were full of blisters so I was walking in my reflexology-spiked flip-flops. I knew I was not going to be walking for long. In fact, I asked Matt to be excused from walking at all, but they needed all bodies for the film, as too few co-walkers showed up that morning.

We walked about one-half of a mile with the monks and I decided I needed to turn around and go back to my car. A few of my friends decided to follow me. As we began to depart from the monks, the oldest one in Japanese said something to us to convey that he wanted to pray over us first. So he led the monks in what seemed like a long, beautiful blessing prayer for us, raising and lowering his hands over us as he said his prayers. I was touched to tears and kept feeling shivers running up and down my body by the powers of their intention. As we parted, my friends and I were so moved that we could not speak.

Just several yards away from the monks, as we continued to walk back toward our cars, now about 5:30 a.m. a friendly jogger ran up from behind us and said, "Good morning!" Instantly in my head I heard a loud, "Stop him!" Arguing with myself inside of my own head, my mind said to me, "What a weird thought. I am not going to stop a jogger in the middle of a run..." Just then one of my friends said we needed someone to take our picture under the famous Praying Monk Rock Formation of Camelback Mountain, directly above us. So then I thought to myself, "I must have had a premonition of that and so I am supposed to stop that jogger..."" "Hey!" I yelled out to the jogger who was now at least fifty yards beyond us, "Can you take our picture?" Startled, he turned around and said, "Sure."

He began walking with us after the picture taking and having noticed Terri's "Department of Peace T-Shirt," he mentioned that he had read about the monk's walk and the Department of Peace Initiative in the newspaper. He continued to talk about how much he and his family from Santa Fe had been involved in various peace movements. He said, "I have written and played songs about peace all of my life." We were walking in a pricy neighborhood where people frequently bragged about things. Not impressed, I said in an obligatory way, "Like what songs?" He looked at me with an almost shy, embarrassed way and he said, "Well, I have written a bunch of songs, maybe you have heard of *Fly Like an Eagle*?"To which I replied, "The whole world has heard of *Fly Like an Eagle* and if I remember right, it was Steve Miller who wrote that song and you aren't Steve Miller."

Steve's version of the story today, is that about this time he was going to wave good-bye and just say, "Have a nice day." But for whatever reason, he stayed. He said, "Steve Miller is my partner and has been for many years, and we wrote a bunch of songs together." Still not believing him, who knows why I wanted to keep challenging him, "If you wrote that song, why don't you sing it for us?"

Steve McCarty gave me a not so nice look and said, "I don't sing on demand, and I don't sing anything at 5:30 in the morning." To which I responded, "There, that proves it. If you had written that song, it would come rolling off of your tongue as easily as talking, as many times as you have supposedly sung it."

This is such a weird story because I am not usually like this. But for whatever reason the Heavens were lining up and the Angels were around this God-centered morning, right after one of the most powerful monk encounters of my life, I was about to get to know a different kind of monk.

On the corner of 59th Place and Lincoln, in Paradise Valley, Arizona at 5:30 in the morning as cars whizzed by on their way to another day of work, Steve McCarty, a monk of other colors, belted out, "Fly Like an Eagle" like we had never heard before. Stunned, we all were rushed to tears and joined in singing with him while the people in the cars looked at us like we were crazy.

Terri immediately told Steve that he had to join us in New Mexico for the ceremony, and that it was a sign from God. She said he had to have security clearance immediately and would be joined by Peter Yarrow from Peter, Paul and Mary and Bonnie Raitt (who wasn't able to go after all) and other famous Nobel Prize winning scientists and people. He said, "Ok." He gave his mobile number to Terri who called ahead to Matt to see if we could get Steve an invitation. Matt said that we had to get all of the same security information immediately so he could try to get Steve approved. About ten minutes later Terri called Steve and asked him to give her his social security number, passport, his birth date, and a credit card number. I, being an ex-banker was horrified that we might be considered identity theft collaborators. Steve said, "Just a minute" and proceeded to give Terri enough information to obtain his identity and security clearance.

We all met in Albuquerque, New Mexico together with the monks, film crew and other invitees on August 9 to board the buses, escorted by government security, at the Drury Inn to make the two-hour road trip to the Trinity military site. The rain, thunder and lightning had been pounding the city all day. We were told that if lightning was striking when we arrived at the site, we would not be able to enter because it would be too dangerous. They told us the land still had leftover radioactive substances that could possibly conduct electrical current. Subdued, each of us in our own way prayed that we would be able to enter the site.

It was a surreal bus ride. Steve McCarty sat in one seat. Right in front of Maren and me was Peter Yarrow singing, "Puff the Magic Dragon" and "Where Have All the Flowers Gone?" in between working on computer for his blog about peace. The monks were sitting at the front of the bus and several scientists were discussing their work toward making the world safer. It continued to rain hard, thunder and strike lightning. Our buses kept going.

It was just nearing sunset when we crossed over the cattle guards onto the Trinity Site and suddenly all rain and lightening stopped. A large black cloud that filled the entire sky seemed to hover over us but actually lifted, causing a gap between the distant mountains and the black cloud above to let a small window of blue sky show on us as we left the buses and began our silent march toward the small monument marking the site where the first atomic bomb was placed on a 100-foot steel tower and exploded.

The ceremony was beautiful and appropriate. The Zen Monks were constantly mumbling quiet prayers while creating a circle of pillows around the front of the monument. They unfolded a large white cloth onto the ground in the center of the circle and they placed one thousand colorful Origami folded paper cranes, made by children in Japan, symbolizing their wish for peace to come true, in the center of the cloth. The one hundred or so of the rest of us stood in a larger circle, completely silent as we observed and took part in this most Holy experience. Among several famous people were mothers who had lost children exposed to nuclear testing in Nevada and Utah and veterans of World War II. The black cloud above us was completely quiet; no wind, no discernable movement of the cloud, it was as if even all of Heaven was hushed in this healing memorial service. I felt connected and humbled to see the entire human, spiritual and natural world symbolically and truly linked together in that moment.

The monks knelt on the pillows and continued to pray for a while and then they stood, forming a line between the monument and the circle they had created. One of the monks opened the lantern holding the live flame and knelt down to light the white cloth, which immediately burst into flames, engulfing the paper cranes. As we watched this fire quickly extinguish the white prayer cloth and paper birds, the flame began to flicker as it too, was dying, until it ceased to burn any longer. The Atomic Flame was now extinguished and returned back to its source. Just then, the sun dropped from behind the dark cloud to begin its ascent behind the mountains just prior to sunset. The rays of the sun immediately hit our faces as if to say, "It is done." The monks began to gently and quietly gather the ashes from the burn to deposit them into an ancient wooden chest, full of ashes gathered from the original bombsites at Hiroshima and Nagasaki. The combined ashes would be taken back to Japan to eventually be distributed to many corners of the world as a prayerful reminder.

Everyone boarded the buses silently. Everyone was full of emotion. Several peoples' faces were still wet with quiet tears. So many thoughts and prayers consumed us all. We each took our seats and the buses began to move toward the exit gate. It was now almost dark outside. As the wheels of our bus crossed the cattle guard of the gate, the rain started with a bolt of lightning. The storm followed us back to Albuquerque.

Steve McCarty was sitting across the aisle from me and after about an hour began to talk to me. As we were trying to speak in a quiet tone across the aisle, I moved to his seat so that we could talk easier. We were married a year later. He has become one of StarShine's greatest ambassadors, head of the music school, and has become a great reservoir of support and help for me. It's nice to have music in the house.

13

STARSHINE GOES GLOBAL

The world has changed dramatically, with globalization and free trade, moving from an industrial economy to an information economy, ... But while that's been happening, K-12 education hasn't changed at all. Meanwhile, China's graduating five times as many engineers as we are, and you look at India and you get alarmed. ----Eli Broad

Each year since we opened in 2002, Joe Martori hosted all of the high school kids during Christmastime in Sedona, Arizona at his ILX Resorts, Los Abrigados and Bell Rock. The resorts were decorated with Christmas lightshow contests featuring local artists and hobbyists and Joe and Mia, our board member, wanted the kids to share in the delight of the season.

The kids were pampered in every way. In the evening in Sedona after the two hour ride from Phoenix, a decorated trolley would pick them up for their fancy dinner after they all got dressed up in pretty dresses, coats and ties. For most of the kids, they had never been outside of Phoenix or to a nice restaurant. Some of the students had never seen a pine tree or received a Christmas present. During the breakfast the next day, the kids got presents from Santa and his helper, Elf.

Each year, several adult volunteer friends of mine made the trip with me to help chaperone the kids and help them to tie ties and get the clothes they needed. The kids felt and looked elegant. People at the resorts thought they were from a private school because the kids had such impeccable manners and kindness. We took the kids on long Eco walks with the Institute of EcoTourism and picked up trash while learning about ancient medicinal plants in the forest. And they learned about the magnificent Grand Canyon close by.

Sedona became a magical place of healing for the kids. Joe gave them each a book he wrote about his own upbringing called *Street Fights* and each year would talk to the kids about his childhood and how success is made. Every year, at least one student would come back from that trip completely changed. One year it happened to me and shortly afterward, StarShine began to change.

It was a few months after Christmastime, in March of 2005; Mia wanted the Institute of EcoTourism in Sedona to invite world class authors, scientists and sustainability experts to come together for a symposium about building sustainable communities. Vernon Swaback had written his book *Creative Communities* and was invited to be one of the featured speakers. The people attending and participating in the seminar were who's who of environmentalists trying, at the time to get the public to pay attention to the environment. It wasn't quite trendy yet. StarShine was considered a sustainable-teaching school

The night before the symposium, Mia, Joe and I went to dinner together to discuss the next day's events. I left to return to my room fairly early in the evening as I had some writing to do to prepare for the symposium. Sedona is so beautiful and this evening was no different. It had started to rain lightly and a soft feathery fog-cloud was hovering just below the cliffs near the hotel, causing a silver glow just outside of my patio.

I went to bed around ten o'clock, but I woke up again at 3:33a.m. and couldn't go back to sleep. I got up and opened my patio door to let the smell of the drizzling rain come into the room. The birds started singing in the bushes outside of my patio. This was very strange, as it was dark and raining, which usually would mean the birds are asleep. I was very curious about all of this so I started to write in my journal. I then decided to turn on the stacked CD player in the room and pushed the random CD setting. The first song that came on was John Lennon, *Imagine*. This too, seemed too much of a coincidence, but then the next song was Judy Collins, *Amazing Grace*. After five more songs with a similar, "Save the World" theme, I knew something unusual was about to happen. I became tired and so decided to go back to bed for a couple of hours of sleep.

Almost immediately, I fell into a deep sleep and intense dream. My body; I could feel it, I was in it, not just watching it, but I could also see it, was catapulted up to the top of a tall ceiling with wooden beams and a huge central crystal chandelier that was sparkling with so much light and vast colors, it seemed as if it would hurt my eyes, but it didn't. The light and the colors were flooding and piercing my body as it bathed me in the most beautiful, soft feeling of trust and contentment. I was listening to my breathing and feeling the color as the most beautiful music I have ever heard began to play. It was as if every angel, every harp and all classical music came together in total harmony and began to gently fill my ears in delicious sound. I remember saying to myself, "this music is not from this world. I can feel it as it moves through me and I can feel the colors." I continued to float under the chandelier, up above my bed, as the music began to soften and the most incredible woman's gentle voice began to speak to me in a language I could not understand. I knew in my heart and in my head this was Holy Mother Mary, even though I am not Catholic, I knew this. I even said to myself in the dream, "Oh great, this is Mother Mary giving me a message I can't understand."

She continued to speak to me although I never saw her or the music. When she finished, the music began to fade and after a few seconds completely disappeared. The colors and the light began to pale as I was gently brought back down to my bed. It seemed like I awoke immediately as my eyes opened and were wet with tears. I had been crying in my dream. It was still dark outside, with the same clouds and the birds still singing. It was one of the strongest, most profound dreams I have had, although I still search for the meaning. StarShine almost immediately began to change.

As StarShine continued to grow and began to catch attention, we tried to keep things as quiet as possible; not much fanfare or publicity because of two things:

1. We wanted to make sure it was working and not just a lucky guess.

2. Conspiracy or not, there were many self-interest groups searching for and destroying great school ideas and we did not want to be sidetracked in having to deal with them.

We were gaining much support for our work from the various accountability and compliance groups coming in to check on us, especially through much of the Arizona Department of Education and the AdvancEd Accreditation teams. Word was leaking out that we had some sort of magical way of turning kids around to become academically engaged, disciplined and successful. It wasn't magic, it was logical specific strategies, working together that seemed to create magic.

Dignitaries attended our graduation ceremonies each year. The Arizona Republic Newspaper wrote a front page article about one of our students and how hard it was for her to find her way to graduate, until she found StarShine. I had no idea the article was being done so was surprised when my phone started ringing. Our reputation was growing in spite of my desire to go unnoticed for a while.

You are always a more sought-after expert the further away you are from home. And that is what happened to StarShine and to me. I was asked to go to Regina, Canada with Ian Percy, one of the top Transformational Leader Presenters, to be a featured speaker at the League of Educational Administrators, Directors and Superintendents of Saskatchewan in October of 2005. They wanted me to talk about the strategies we used to produce changes we were discovering through working with the students and teachers at StarShine. Canada's leadership has a reputation for always seeking out best ideas and solutions and they had heard about and wanted to learn from us. Things started to snowball shortly afterward and we were asked to consult with people and schools everywhere.

In May of 2009 we went to Shanghai with the AdvancED Accreditation and CITA, the Commission on International and Trans-Regional Accreditation, to meet with many world education, political and business leaders. I was truly astounded by the reverence Chinese people had and the longing they had, to learn about and visit the

United States. They especially revere American education. We spent several days talking with university representatives and touring schools for young children. It really opened my eyes about the importance of an American education and how it impacts the rest of the world. I had been indoctrinated to believe that China's education system was somehow better and that the students are much more serious and much more well behaved learners. But while in a private conversation with the minister of education, with the aid of his translator, he explained to me how worried he is for his country's future. He said that generally Chinese kids spend hours memorizing facts but cannot analyze or systematize complicated pieces of information to come to conclusions. Engineers, he said, do analytic and deductive reason, with superior results from the United States, but not China, even though they graduate many more engineers than the U.S.. He explained that most of the students want to move away from farming into the cities, causing their food supply chain at risk. He gave me several examples of huge errors that had been made in recent times, because no one thought to question something. "They left out the bathrooms in a large-scale stadium because no one noticed," his translator conveyed to me. "Would you come here and help us to teach more entrepreneurism in our schools?" he asked me. I felt sad as I explained that the culture in China encourages kids NOT to ask questions, and asking questions is the basis of learning to think.

Meeting with several Chinese students and watching them use their computers, the Chinese version of Skype and their cell phones, gave me an idea that things in China are rapidly changing. I found several kids with hidden tattoos and tongue piercings. I asked a few of them if they were afraid to become independent thinkers in "Communist China." Most of the students laughed at my naiveté. They assured me that they are just like kids everywhere. I watched Chinese television to see shows that looked very much like American television. I saw soap operas and variety shows. I saw something that looked like a talent contest and I watch Chinese girls doing cheers that resembled any high school cheerleading group in the U.S. I drank coffee at Starbucks where I watched the employees participate in a coffee tasting that resembled a ceremonial tea tasting.

I came back from that China trip with more determination than ever to concentrate as much of my own efforts as possible on helping to achieve a wide scale change in the way we educate our American kids, knowing how much our culture and our education philosophy effects the rest of our world. We must do everything in our power to do the best we can. Everything that has made our country's education system one of the best in the world seems to me to be at a fast risk of failure.

14

AFRICA WILL CHANGE THE
UNITED STATES

Success is peace of mind which is a direct result of self-satisfaction in knowing you made the effort to become the best of which you are capable."
--John Wooden

I was visiting my mom in Durango, Colorado with my husband, Steve in July of 2009, when I received one of the most unusual calls of my life. I was invited to travel with a small group to Monrovia, Liberia to conduct the largest teacher training ever to be provided in Africa. I was asked by a humanitarian group called Humanity Unites Brilliance and a group in Liberia led by international leader, Kimmie Weeks, called Youth Action International,
    http://www.youthactioninternational.org .
They had heard of us because the year before, StarShine Academy had opened a Phoenix test pilot for refugee students, a one-year K-12 school as an outreach with a church helping refugee children and word about it had traveled back to Liberia. We had several children from Liberia in our school in northern Phoenix and at one time had sixty-eight languages spoken at the one school. (We used IPhones for translating.) Because Liberia had been at war for over twenty years the country was in dire need of schools and teacher training. Having had our experience teaching our own refugee children, especially from Liberia, we had developed a comfort and system with working with children from different tribes, customs and languages.

On the call requesting us to go to Liberia, they also told me that we needed to put our entire K-12 curriculum into one book that could fit into a backpack, because most of the teachers had so few resources. Behind these requests was Liberia's president, Ellen Johnson Sirleaf, a Harvard educated woman, and the first woman in Africa to become president as she came into power in 2005. The mayor of Monrovia,

Liberia, Mary Broh, the first female mayor in Africa and we were scheduled to meet together. The training was to take place in the town hall of the city of Monrovia.

The phone call seemed surreal, as did the trip in our car, toward Phoenix on the way back from Durango, the next day. Steve and I drove through the ancient Holy lands of the Southwest Tribal Nations, and Four Corners near Shiprock, New Mexico and Kayenta, Arizona. We talked the whole way back about Africa, America and changing education for all children. And we discussed what we knew of the predictions from the Zuni and Hopi Tribes over four thousand years ago, that the world would change and peace would come out of the four corners area of the United States, predicted before there were any states.

I was concerned about trying to figure out how to put our entire curriculum into one book so was madly making lists of things not to forget. Steve, in the meantime, named it, being the Wordsmith he is, *"StarShine Field Schools Teacher Training Manual."* It seemed like a dream.

As we began to read and learn everything we could about Liberia, we became more excited about our upcoming trip. I watched a documentary movie that had been shown on PBS in 2008, produced by Abigail Disney called *"Pray the Devil Back to Hell"* chronicling a small group of women led by Leymah Gbowee and Janet Johnson Bryant, who brought peace to the country, allowing President Sirleaf to come into power. Ms. Gbowee won the Nobel Peace Prize last year. The film is one of the most important films I have ever seen, inspiring the message that one person can change everything.

Ms. Gbowee was mocked and called "pathetic" by investigative reporters who refused to write about her during the war because she would never be able to "make a difference." She believed mothers were the only pathway to peace. One night, she awoke from a dream where God had told her, "Gather the women and pray for peace!" She thought it was a message for her to give to someone else. She had organized one hundred women to wear a uniform of white T-shirts and who promised to refuse sex, even if they had to die, until the war stopped. "We are tired of war. We are tired of running. We are tired of begging for bulgur wheat. We are tired of our children being raped. We are now taking this stand, to secure the future of our children. Because we believe, as custodians of society, tomorrow our children will ask us, 'Mama, what was your role during the crisis?"

As I researched Liberia and these courageous women, I knew I was meant to go, but I was still terrified. The country was still in trouble and it was so far away from my home and StarShine Academy in Arizona. "Who am I to do this?" I continually asked myself. And then I would remind myself of my friend's quote, Marianne Williamson,

> "Our deepest fear is not that we are inadequate. Our deepest fear is that we are powerful beyond measure. It is our light, not our darkness that most frightens us. We ask ourselves, Who am I to be brilliant, gorgeous, talented, fabulous? Actually, who are you not to be? You are a child of God. Your playing small does not serve the world. There is nothing enlightened about shrinking so that other people won't feel insecure around you. We are all meant to shine, as children do. We were born to make manifest the glory of God that is within us. It's not just in some of us; it's in everyone. And as we let our own light shine, we unconsciously give other people permission to do the same. As we are liberated from our own fear, our presence automatically liberates others."

I also read *The House at Sugar Beach* by Helene Cooper, White House correspondent for the New York Times; the book was written to describe her life as a young child growing up in Liberia before and during the war. I found myself entranced by the stories about Liberia and what Liberia had meant to the United States. The natural resources there are abundant. It has one of the largest rainforests of timber, diamond, gold and iron ore deposits, as well as oil. The Firestone Family had the largest rubber plantations in the world and had begun several business partnerships since 1926 with the Liberian people. The civil war had devastating effects on these businesses as it did for all living in Liberia. (Fascinating now that Cinda Firestone is my editor of this book and believes it is of great importance.)

Liberia has a fascinating history tied to the United States as former United States slaves founded it in 1847. Most of the people of Liberia speak English and many are educated because prior to the war, there had been established an economy based on U.S. economics. Liberia had the most universities and schools of any African country.

But the split between the "Haves and Have-nots" created a combustible circumstance for unrest that eventually led to one of the most devastating and long-lasting civil wars. Riots occurred in the 1970s and eventually escalated to a civil war that erupted in 1989 and continued to 2003, killing over 200,000 Liberians and sending another one million to refugee camps. The civil war used many children as soldiers and after a twenty year history of fighting, the country is literally torn apart.

I wrote the following blog one evening from my hotel room as we were providing the training and my heart was heavy:

Field School Teacher Training August 22, 2009

"The Liberians are a proud people. They don't dance, sing and carry-on in public unless it is in church on Sunday morning," the young Liberian political leader and founder of Youth Action International,

Kimmie Weeks, told me. It is Saturday evening on the beach in Liberia, as we sit at our table and enjoy one of our last evenings in this most unusual place.

We see one star, a ton of beach trash, and barbed-razor wire fencing around our hotel. We laugh and talk about how much we like the Liberian version of English...a kind of Creole, with a French twist while speaking English words, with a yaya at the end of each sentence, even if one word. Beautiful. It almost sounds musical.

We ended the three-day training yesterday evening and, for the first time since our arrival, it began to rain. I stood out in the drizzle along with the cameraman and Spryte Loriano from Humanity Unites Brilliance, talking about what happened here, as a fitting ending of a most mystical, magical three days. We talked about how more people crowded into the last few hours, just to hear a little more. Kimmie remarked, "You know, usually on a three day training like this, on the first day, all the people come, the second day one-half come back, on the third morning about one-half again show up, and by Friday afternoon we are lucky to see 20 or 30 people. I have never seen anything like this. We had people trying to crowd in even in the last few minutes."

The StarShine Academy Field School Teacher Training focused on peace building skills, brain exercises for peak efficiency, and social etiquette interwoven in financial literacy. The Liberians, 600-800 of them—we were never really sure—were listening so intently that at times I prayed that I would say the right things that they needed to hear. On Friday morning, the four of us girls walked onto the stage in our colorful, full-garb, African dresses, as a means of connecting and honoring the audience to the last day of the seminar.

The crowd went wild, as they did when we ran out of books in the beginning and out of graduation certificates at the end. We ordered more books and we were able to get more graduation certificates printed still in time for Friday night. I have never felt this much love and appreciation from this large of a crowd. The Liberians are smiling and sweet. They are happy most of the time, even though most of them live in poverty that many of us in the United States would find appalling.

They walk with the pride of soldiers, not only to show their love of their country and their pride in themselves, but also because so many of these people were stolen as young children to fight in a war that they did not understand, using weapons that they had never before seen. And now they are teachers, leading the way out of poverty and devastation from the wars of the past twenty years, they make an average of between $20 per month and $70 per month in U.S. dollars. And yet our hotel bill here is $200+ per night and our dinners average $25 per meal.

The potential in Liberia is immense. They have diamonds, a huge rainforest that will be providing trees for other countries, Firestone Rubber Plantations, Chinese-owned iron ore, and a beautiful ocean (if you ignore the trash.) These teachers have learned that education is what makes cash assets. And if you live right, cash assets make the world a better place. This experience has been incredibly complicated and yet one of the blessings of my life. The people believe that their country will be the leader for many things, but in particular, the way that they educate and care for their children.

As I looked around today at the little children, as young as five years old, fetching water for their family from the town water supply, a manual pump and faucet in the center of the village, I remind myself not to cry. These children, I tell myself, are the lucky ones. They are fetching the water. They have enough to eat and they are living in a country that values education above all other things, I hope. There are many other children, too weak to do much of anything.

I am grateful for this opportunity to spend time with the Liberian teachers and principals and to get to know the culture briefly. These people are proud. I smile as I picture all of us dancing to "Mama Liberia" and singing peace out into the ethers of the world, to reach every ear, so that this kind of hope, enthusiasm and appreciation continues into the future forever.

- Trish McCarty Signing Off from Liberia

Even in one of the poorest countries, Liberia, these people understand true assets. They explained to me what they call "Shiny Eyes" as a way to tell whether a person has love, truth or trust, or not. They said you only must look at whether or not a person has "Shiny Eyes" to know truth and love. I made a vow during that trip to work with every child and every teacher until I can see shiny eyes.

The Nobel Peace Prizes recognized the bravery exhibited by the women leaders of this country and other countries in Africa, toward a better life for their children, in 2011. Liberian Nobel Peace Prize winners President Ellen Johnson Sirleaf, and peace activist Leymah Gbowee, were inspired to pray and protest for peace during Liberia's civil war, in Monrovia, Liberia, and throughout Liberia. In the documentary *"Pray the Devil Back to Hell"* Ms. Gbowee was described as "pathetic" by the press who noted that there was no way this one small person could ever make a difference against so many odds and so much destruction, when in fact, she changed history. "if you're hungry, keep walking. If you're thirsty, keep walking. If you want a taste of freedom, keep walking. For us women of Liberia, this award is a call that we will keep walking until peace, justice and the justice and rights of women is not a dream, but a thing of the present," said Gbrowee as she was presented with the Profile of Courage award. I encourage you to take fourteen minutes and watch her inspiring speech as she accepted her Nobel Prize:

http://www.nobelprize.org/mediaplayer/index.php?id=1749

The experience in Liberia caused several pivotal changes to our work at StarShine and increased our desire to achieve our original mission of StarShine even faster; *StarShine will change education for every child on the planet.*

When we were asked to go to Liberia, and also asked to put our entire K-12 curriculum into one book that could fit into a backpack; it didn't even make sense. At first, I thought this would be an impossible thing to do as I pictured in my mind, the libraries full of curriculum that we currently have in use, and trying to fit them all into one book. But the more I thought about it, the more I wanted to try to meet this challenge. Filter down to simple ideas... I kept thinking.

I decided to implement easy mathematics. What if we were to begin with the end in mind? What would a student have to know to get into a top-rated college? And what would a student have to know to be able to maintain an accredited education?

We met together with top curriculum experts from Arizona State University and Maricopa Community Colleges and posed the same problem. Most of our genius expert advisors came together to help. What would we have to put into one book if that is the only book that a student or teacher would have access to, in order to eventually give them the foundation to get into college?

We did not have more than a few weeks to formulate this one book that we could use in Liberia. But we did it! We put together a *StarShine Field School Teacher Training Manual* that includes charts, graphs, lists, maps, brain training, health guides, student management systems and school procedures and formulas of information that a student would have to understand if they wanted to go to college. We did it using guidelines for core academic standards, International Baccalaureate Standards and our StarShine Academy AdvancED Accreditation. We wanted it to provide a guide to teachers that would be consistent throughout all StarShine schools, whether in Africa or the United States, whether learning on dirt or on a computer. We included StarShine processes for creating themes for learning based on national and international holidays and we included language and science rules. We included Dolch word lists because 70% or more of the English language is made up of two hundred twenty or so words, insuring that if a child learns how to spell and read those words, they can usually figure out other English words. And we included simple manners. It includes a chart to formalize a student's ILP; Individual Learning Plan and a monthly guide to allow all StarShine students to share experiences based on themes. It would provide a global learning grid that kids could share no matter where they are.

We were more than thrilled with our production of our masterpiece book and have only slightly revised it since then. The *StarShine Field Schools Teacher Training Manual* has now been taught and used in at least fifteen countries, as a means to simplify K-12 policy, research and compliance while supporting K-12 academics, innovation and creativity and teacher effectiveness and impact.

As the United Kingdom began to work on their free school movement similar to our charter school movement, we were called upon to travel there to provide the same *StarShine Field Schools Teacher Training Manual* teacher and school training. This time, though, was going to be a first-class trip as the training was provided at the world famous Broughton Castle, in Banbury, Oxfordshire, very near Oxford College. We worked with sophisticated, well-healed and well-educated teachers, administrators, counselors and business people.

Broughton Castle is stunning and considered to be one of the most beautiful castles in England, built in 1300. It had been the site of one of the first Oxford Colleges and had hosted the Knights of the Roundtable as well as several modern movies. The same family has occupied Broughton since the time it was built. One of the rooms is called "Room that Hath no Ears" and was the place where noble men and dignitaries met in 1629 to begin plans to overthrow the king. Our Australian partner, Dr. John Findlay, founder of Zing Technologies came with us. We all agreed that this was very synergistic that we were at the helm of a revolution in education in the U.K. in a castle that at one time housed a man responsible for launching what would become one of the most revered colleges in the world, Oxford.

Strongly, I found this experience very similar to our experience in China and in Liberia, as weird as that may seem. Such different cultures in the three countries, in opposite ends of the world, each group taking care of us in very unique ways. We were dignitaries to the people hosting us in these foreign countries, so the people did everything they could to make our time spent as enjoyable as possible. In China, we stayed in a Five-Star Hotel and ate food especially prepared for us. In Liberia, we stayed in an upscale hotel but not much better than a cheap hotel in America, it was the safest they had. The training was done in their best and biggest building with broken windows, one electrical cord that dangled from the ceiling and water dripping in through the roof with mold over much of the inside of the walls. And now here we were in a castle in England, staying in a boutique hotel that looked like it was made for Hansel and Gretel in a fairytale.

I was so surprised to hear different people in these three countries describing their children, their desire for education and their lives in very similar ways. Everyone wants the best for the children, no matter where you go. And describing what is "the best" is pretty common sense thinking: they want their children to grow up to be able to work and enjoy life and to be healthy. And everywhere I went, the people love the United States and what the American Dream is in their minds. I realized that more people outside of the United States agree with what the American Dream is than Americans. I think if we asked one hundred American citizens to describe the American Dream, we would get nearly one hundred answers. I just want the American Dream to grow and not to fall apart. So I rededicated our efforts to fix things at home first, if we could just stay ahead of the demand from offshore.

It was enticing to travel so much, so I had a hard decision turning opportunities away for a while. We were treated better and paid well, further from home. In Arizona, we constantly had to dodge criticism and argue about why culture in a school is more important than the math curriculum. The status quo for NOT changing education can be tough when you are trying to "fix" something that has been far too broken for far too long, taking no agenda or influence from politics or self-interest groups. There was always someone lurking around wanting to force us to do it his or her way, or encouraging us to give up. But our way at StarShine was working because it was all about doing the right thing with the right heart: the kids' needs, nothing else, other than staying legal. And legal doesn't necessarily protect the kids either; it might be for something else. So we decided to stay home for a while and try to help other American towns and states.

15

BACK TO THE USA

OUR BRAINS, OUR HAPPINESS AND OUR COUNTRY

"There is nothing more difficult to take in hand, more perilous to conduct, or more uncertain in its success, than to take the lead in the introduction of a new order of things."
— Niccolo Machiavelli *The Prince (1532)*

We decided to take at least one year and not travel or give speeches, but look at everything we were doing to see how we might improve and to write everything down. I felt like we were getting too popular without having enough of the answers. And we did not have the technology in place to be able to help all of the people asking, so I also wanted to get that fixed.

My mom has always called me the Crystal Turtle and gave one to me for my desk to remind me that it is okay to want to slow down as long as you keep moving forward. I know that today that seems to be counter-intuitive, but I felt that we needed to get things right before going too much more into the market. We had a lot of kids in our own schools and they too, needed our undivided attention.

We spent the better part of the next year almost re-engineering everything we had previously done. I wanted a system that would never again become stuck, but would continually improve as students, teachers and parents used it. I wanted it to break if someone used it for anything other than to help a student achieve his or her own dreams and aspirations. And I wanted it built on a technology platform that anyone can get to, anytime they have access to any technology. I wanted anyone who uses StarShine's brain to be able to very easily and pleasantly access exactly what their brain needed and wanted, and I wanted it to be in real time, just like Facebook or Google.

Being always inquisitive, I spent hours and hours on the Internet, along with Dr. Davies, to research each of our models to see if anything had greatly improved lately. I found some really helpful sites to help us to come up with better answers. Had we been able to, I certainly would have used outside expertise. We did not have the money to be able to hire outside consultants to help us, so we had to find information that we could use.

We rewrote our business plan and looked at each page for any way to improve it. We had grown a lot and experienced what students had taught us in our own school as well as in international schools. Our mission and most of our initial work was still relevant, but everything needed fresh eyes and more statistics.

By then, because of much of our work, most schools were at least talking about individualizing education and teaching the "whole" child. More schools were starting to install some sort of gardening program and people were beginning to be more serious about teaching "real-world" curriculum. Although the arts and physical education programs continued to suffer, at least more articles were being written about it. We were starting to feel like time had begun to catch up with us, and the national desire to change education was beginning to cross our paths at just the right moment.

We were now seeing more and more examples of decentralized organizations growing exponentially. We were also seeing more venture money funding business doing good work for the planet, instead of the opposite. Things were truly looking up.

We found an incredible tool at the Institute of Design at Stanford called the *"d.school bootcamp bootleg."* The process is built from collaborators throughout the world and is used as a living, working document to help business to better design themselves. They have come up with what they call "D.MINDSETS;" seven ways to help build a human-centered process for system design and then they have a toolkit which support these.

The seven D.Mindsets are:

1. Show don't tell
2. Create clarity from complexity
3. Be mindful of process
4. Collaborate across boundaries
5. Bias toward action
6. Get experimental and experiential
7. Focus on human values

I found these extremely helpful in taking a deeper look at what was going on at StarShine, but I also thought they could be a great list for a family trying to improve. They deeply emphasized keeping a beginners mindset without preconceived mindsets, opinions, experiences or assumptions. Explaining how to achieve and maintain a beginners

mindset started with a simple list:
— Don't judge
— Question everything
— Be truly curious
— Find patterns
— Listen. Really

Can you imagine what kind of a relationship we could have with a teenager or a small child if we stayed in a "Beginners mindset?" We could immediately improve the quality of our own lives and the quality of the lives of the people around us. Living this way would open one door after another of potentially joyous living.

As we all participated in several StarShine Translational Change meetings we used a few simple rules. One that was taught to me by some of the native people living near Phoenix is called the Talking Stick. It is a beautiful stick that is passed to the one doing the talking. Whomever has the stick, is the only one allowed to talk, no matter how important an idea someone else may have, they must wait for a turn to have the stick. We have used a version of this many times with the kids. We might use a rock or something else they like, maybe sitting in a particular chair. It teaches listening and honoring. We use it in our family, especially if discussing something particularly difficult.

And we always encourage the wildest ideas…coming from my past with AT&T, wild ideas are what made the Bell Labs famous; that and figuring out how to make them a reality.

During this "thinking and doing" year we met Betsy Hill and Roger Stark who founded *BrainWare SAFARI/ Learning Enhancement Corporation*. This was a quantum leap for StarShine and perhaps their organization. We were kindred in our desire to change K-12 education and to deliver the highest available tools, but we were different in our focus. Perfect!

They have spent years developing fun, engaging, interactive software designed to improve the ability of a brain to learn. They had evidence of extensive testing on their approaches to cognitive (mental processing) skill development aimed at improving attention, memory, visual processing, auditory processing, sensory integration and thinking.

Scientific research has demonstrated that the brain is constantly able to change and that with the right training it develops new and stronger neural connections, no matter a person's age. Although StarShine's hunch was to work with the potential of each child, we now had proof of some of the processes we could use to prove that, not only was it possible, there was a enormous proof that it worked. Students having previous behavior/discipline issues and pre-tested 3 years behind their age goup, after just 11 weeks on Safari, had increased their performance by 6 years.

We also met another Rock Star of education, Dr. Robert Marzano. He has written so many books and is revered by so many educators, he is what Donald Trump is to business, and he is of education. He has spent his life doing research on what works and then writing and speaking about it. When I met him, he was in a bit of a mental slump. He told me that he has sold millions of books and not made a difference in K-12 education. I assured him StarShine uses everything he has. We decided to work together to help each other change the world of K-12 education.

16

VALUES, NOT RULES: STARSHINE FIFTEEN GUIDING PRINCIPALS

"It is the perfection of God's works that they are all done with the greatest simplicity. He is the God of order and not of confusion. And therefore as they would understand the frame of the world must endeavor to reduce their knowledge to all possible simplicity, so must it be in seeking to understand these visions"
-Sir Isaac Newton

Developing the StarShine Fifteen Guiding Principles took several years as we tried to come up with what we thought would be our long-term agreements for going forward. We asked the parents, the students, the volunteers, and elders in the surrounding neighborhood, as well as business leaders and many experts, to give us their own opinions about what Guiding Principles should look like for a replicable school, StarShine. We agreed after working and reworking them over and over again that they would guide our decisions, our actions, and our partnerships and would give us the very basis of what our schools would reflect.

Principle-based organizations create buy-in because people "choose" to agree with the principles. Rules, on the other hand typically make people want to do something else. If you think about comparisons, you might consider a 55 mile-an-hour speed limit "rule" or law, versus the principle behind the Autobahn in Germany where no speed limit exists but the principle is to be safe. More accidents are experienced on roads where the 55 mile-per-hour rules exist than on the Autobahn.

We wanted to create a system of buy-in at every level; from the students, parents, teachers and community. There are rules that govern everything in education, so StarShine wanted to create a winning example of why a student would want to be a great example. Hence the Fifteen Guiding Principles of StarShine were born in January of 2006.

STARSHINE GUIDING PRINCIPLE #1.

Every person born is unique and perfect and on their own road to discovering their dreams and highest calling.

At StarShine we believe that every child has a unique way to discover, to learn, and to contribute and that woven together with the rest of the world, he or she makes the world what it should be. Every child is born as a perfect receptor for future possibilities. If we would look at children as unique possibilities to make the world a better place, perhaps we would each take greater care of all of our children and their education.

Jairo

In the eyes of the judge and the prosecutors, the evidence was irrefutable. As the judge prepared to pronounce sentence, I rose to my feet with my heart pounding and my feelings in my throat.

"Your honor, may I speak in his behalf?"

* * * * * *

Jairo had been one of the first students to show up at StarShine. Because it usually took awhile to obtain records, we were enrolling anyone who came to our door. Jairo was Hispanic, tall, good-looking and smart. He spoke English well, but it was obvious that he was tough and street-savvy. He was seventeen years old, almost an adult, and a smart aleck, annoying teachers who tried to work with him. We appeared to make little headway with him despite employing every tactic we could find.

Yet, at that point, we were discovering that everyone wants someone to believe in him or her and a chance to believe in themselves. In fact, there are only three things that govern all human judgment:

- Am I lovable?
- Am I relevant?
- Am I significant?

Everybody wants to leave a mark. In Jairo's life his experience taught him that he was not lovable, relevant or significant, unless he was in trouble. His father, grandfather, brother, and cousin were all in prison. Jairo had committed his first crime and been arrested at age seven. He had stolen a bicycle at Christmastime because he wanted to learn how to ride. Later he became smarter and more daring, and learned that he could get away with many crimes because he could either outsmart others or charm his way. He'd been in gangs since age eight and had learned how to sell drugs and how to steal cars while people were driving them. It was his survival.

He saw his life as tough, on the street, earning his way up the gang ladder. In his world, he was respected for his fearlessness and didn't mind scaring people with guns. In his mind he was at war with everyone. He had been kicked out of numerous schools since second or third grade, and he told himself that he didn't care, but he really did. Nothing ever made him feel powerful except intimidating others and committing and getting away with crimes.

On one cold, overcast day in November, Jairo came to my office and asked if he could become President of our Lund Family Peace

Garden, the Mustard Seed Garden. (Someone named it that because the mustard seed is the least of seeds, and yet it grows into a huge shrub or a tree. In the Bible too, it says that if you have the faith of a tiny mustard seed, all things are possible. This seemed a good analogy for StarShine.)

I was curious. "Jairo," I asked him, "why do you want to become responsible for the garden?"

"It makes me feel peaceful when I work on it, Miz McCarty," he said, "and it makes me proud to see it taken care of."

"Okay then," I said, "you can be President, but it's going to take a lot of extra time."

A few days later he brought his friend Freddie to meet me and see the garden. Freddie, a shorter version of Jairo, admitted quietly to me that he had been in much gang activity, had dropped out of school long ago, and was now too old to return. Nevertheless, he wanted a connection with us.

"Could I help Jairo on the garden?" he asked.

I explained to them both about the school's responsibility to keep everyone safe and his part, if we let him be on school grounds. We made an agreement that he could help, which included watering and pulling weeds on the weekends. In addition, Freddie began coming in daily just to talk with me for a few minutes. My heart ached for him as I realized that he had never had a normal conversation with anyone.

"You're the first white lady who ever really talked to me," he told me.

Freddie and Jairo worked on the garden every day. We were just starting it and so were fighting weeds and grass and rocks that had accumulated from its years as vacant property. They dug weeds, placed stones in perfect lines, added mulch, and knelt over the garden with their knees stuck in the dirt almost as if praying to the new seeds. They showed up in the dripping rain on the weekends and waited for me to come to unlock the gates.

Nothing ever made him feel truly normal, Jairo told me, *until the garden.* Being able to work with Freddie gave him something he hadn't experienced before - he was creating something positive with a friend, paying it forward, contributing toward someone or something else.

Jairo showed up early for school and stayed late. When he asked me once if he could spend the night on the ground, it saddened me to have to tell him no when I realized that it would probably have been a better place for him than to have to go home. His grades were almost straight A's, he was becoming more helpful and kind to the teachers, and he helped teach the kindergartners how to work in the garden, pointing out to them how leaves turned green from the sun. Jairo's transformation was incredible to watch and a learning experience for me. I had often read how children raised with crime continue in it themselves, but here I was, learning from Jairo and he from me. One day Jairo and Freddie came to my office together. "Do you know any FBI agents?" they asked. When I inquired about their reason, they said, "We'd like to join the FBI someday."

I called a friend who knew two agents and asked if they could come to the school and show the boys how to use our weight equipment. Two handsome, muscular FBI agents showed up and were pleasant to Jairo and Freddie during their session.

When it ended, the agents came to my office, sat down, and asked "Why did you decide to open this school?"

"I think that every kid deserves a chance to excel," I told them, "and I'd like to provide the support and tools to help them accomplish their goals and make the world a better place."

They laughed. One said, "Look at you. You look nothing like what these kids are used to and they have no respect for you or your ideas. There's no way you can make any difference with these kids or any others. When we kick a door down during a drug bust and we see some dirty three-year-old kid crying, sitting on a mattress, we look at him and say, 'You're screwed for life, kid.' It's not their fault. It's just how the world works. Some of us are born the right way and some aren't. We're here to clean the streets of those born into the wrong situation. They will never be anything but a menace to society."

Their words in that moment struck a screeching chord deep within me. It was a turning point in my resolve *never to give up*. These two men were saying our aim was impossible, and it enraged me. It wasn't Jairo and Freddie who had no respect for me, but it was these men, these two know-it-all, been-there-done-that FBI agents.

I'm sure my face was flushed with anger, but I steadied my voice and said to them, "You have the exact same problem these kids have. You've seen so much awful stuff and had so much tough training that it's all you can see. You're blinded by your own judgments and experiences so that you can't see any other possibilities. You guys need to attend this school too and raise your vision, and learn about what you thought was impossible. You're on the firing line where maybe you could grab that three-year-old and help him find another way. Instead you condemn him forever to the life he's sitting in.

"I will be here, and you will see that people can change--any one, any time, with the right information and the right people to help. Someday you'll come back here to this office and apologize for judging me this way. For now, I'd ask that when you see those three year olds sitting on dirty mattresses, you make it your other life's work to get them help."

About two weeks later, I received a chilling call from Jairo. He was sobbing and yelling. The night before, Freddie had been running from someone through back yards after getting off work at 11 p.m., had been stabbed multiple times and died lying in a stranger's back yard in a bad neighborhood. Jairo wanted to find those who did this and make them pay. The phone call jarred me into my own pain and confusion, and I was instantly feeling sorry for myself.

"God," I prayed silently, "I did not sign up for this. It's been hard enough to open a school. I have no experience in dealing with crime like this or helping kids that have to endure pain like this." I can't recall now what I said to Jairo but it seemed to calm him and help him remember his goals in place of getting in trouble.

I went to the funeral and may well have been the only Caucasian there. In the front of the room, near the alter, a white casket holding Freddie's body was open for viewing as seemed to be the custom. The church was packed with kids and adults, some of them crying hysterically. Jairo sat in the middle of two rows of boys, evidently partially in charge. From snatches of words I caught, it seemed to me that they were planning retaliation.

As I sat and listened to one after another walk up onto the church's pulpit to speak about Freddie, my stomach started flipping with butterflies as if pushing me to say something. Many eyes kept looking at me as if it was my duty to pay tribute to Freddie and to say why I was there. The thought of standing in front of these people who I did not know or understand, completely terrified me. I didn't know if they would appreciate it or if I would offend them. I said an earnest prayer to God to help me as I gathered my courage and walked to the front of the little church. Maybe I got the courage because I felt so very sorry for Freddie's mother. As I started shaking, I began to talk from my heart and from my caring for dear Freddie, and for the rest of those kids.

"Let Freddie's death help you realize that you can stop this violence," I said, "by living a life that helps others instead of one that tries to constantly fight others. Creating more violence will only hurt more people. It will never stop until you each decide that you want a better life. There are people like me who will help you, but you must be willing to make the first choice. You each must decide to be more understanding, loving and helpful. You must begin to stand for the life that you want, for peace. Otherwise these tragedies will continue."

The grief and frustration and helplessness of the people in the church made me realize even more how much a school like StarShine could matter to a neighborhood. Afterward Freddy often came to my mind unbidden and I wondered, if he'd been helped and become someone helping people in some distant land, would he still have died this way? Were the two FBI agents right?

Then at the end of December, Jairo came to my office and told me he wouldn't be returning to school.

"I've got five felonies, Miz McCarty, and I've been in school waiting for my court date for sentencing."

I couldn't have been more shocked. I'd had no idea. Five felonies for Jairo seemed impossible.

"There's nothing to do about it," he went on. "I was found guilty already and I've been able to stay out of jail this long by staying in school, so that's what I've been doing."

"Jairo," I said, "I'll go to court and ask them to reconsider."

"Thanks, but it won't matter," he answered.

In January, when Jairo didn't come back, I learned about his court date from the kids and decided to show up. Walking into the court that morning offered learning for me. Jairo sat silently with his mother on the left of the courtroom. On the opposite side were the judge, attorney, and others laughing and talking about their weekend while signing papers. It occurred to me that maybe Jairo was right - what was done was done. The papers being signed would send him to an adult prison.

I rose to my feet and said "Excuse me, your honor, can I say something? I'd like to speak on his behalf."

The judge and attorneys looked up at me with surprised expressions on their faces.

"Who are you?" the judge asked.

"I started the school that Jairo attends and would like to testify for him." The judge agreed to hear me, I was sworn in, and the nearly-empty courtroom settled down to listen to me.

"This is Jairo," I began. "He is a seventeen-year-old boy raised in a way that none of you have ever known or will know. All he has ever known is crime and struggle. He is now the President of our garden and making straight A's. This is the first time in his life that he has been supported to become something more than a liability to society. If you send him to jail, it will cost me as a taxpayer $72,000 a year, and you will live with the memory of me telling you this and wonder what might have happened if you'd given him a chance to become a help to society, a taxpayer."

When I was finished speaking, the judge turned to Jairo.

"Do you have anything to say?" he asked.

The students at StarShine are taught to introduce themselves and to speak directly to audiences, like proud soldiers, so Jairo was ready. He stood up tall and pushed out his chest.

"Judge, sir," he began, "no one has ever believed in me."

He then began to shake and burst out crying. "This school has given me a chance. They think I am good. I just want a chance to be somebody. It is the first time that somebody has ever believed in me."

The judge and lawyers suddenly had tears in their eyes, as did I.

"Jairo," the judge said, "I am going to let you go back to school. If you stay out of trouble until you are twenty-one, I will purge your criminal record completely."

Jairo came back to school and for the most part behaved himself. Some time after he graduated he called to tell me that he'd received "a tax refund for five."

"Five what?" I asked. "Five hundred?"

"No," he said, "five thousand."

I saw him last year at a movie theater box office, in one of the best neighborhoods in Scottsdale, holding the cash drawer behind the glass and wearing a turquoise bow tie.

"Jairo, is that you?" I said.

He came out to talk to me. He'd been working two jobs, one as a manager of that theater. His record had been expunged, and he was attending community college toward one day working for the FBI. He looked happy and healthy, and told me that he still practiced many of the exercises he'd learned at StarShine to stay positive and motivated, and that he always keeps a picture of his goals in his wallet."

If we were taught at the beginning in our families to hold each other accountable to achieve more that we believe, what would our world look like? If our companies paid people to constantly improve and grow wouldn't the companies benefit the most?

STARSHINE GUIDING PRINCIPLE #2.

We are on the planet to help one another toward achieving individual goals for the Greater Good of All.

"I know myself now; and I feel within me, A peace above all earthly dignities, A still and quiet conscience" – William Shakespeare

StarShine believes that we all need one another. On the first day of the school year, everyone meets together in the multi-purpose room. We don't talk about school rules and punishment. We talk about how important the students are as individuals, how they have to help one another and what they need to do to make the world a better place. We work on the StarShine Student Boot Camp for the whole week. We bring in to the room, stacks of magazines, glue, scissors, fancy pens, stamps and poster paper. We tell the kids that they are going to have the most fun at school that they ever have had.

And then we start to make Vision Mind Maps. We tell the students to grab magazines from different subjects and start to flip through the pages. Every time something catches their eye, they are to tear it out and put it in a pile upside down. After about twenty minutes, we tell them to take the pile out and start to cut out pictures of things that caught their attention. These are things that their subconscious mind is attracted to.

Mind maps have been used throughout history, including for Disney and Ben Franklin. We operate and make our daily choices from the conscious mind, but most of the process of judgment is entirely subconscious. This is one of the reasons you tend to make the same mistakes, over and over again. Until you are able to change your access into your deepest thoughts, you continue to live in a world that you are creating by choices that you make subconsciously.

Children, who have been raised in very difficult circumstances, have learned not to dream of better days. In order to begin to open their mind to possibilities, they have to be shown ways to create and dream. In the first few months of the first school, none of the students had ever been on an escalator, yet they all lived in the center of Phoenix! None of them knew that they were allowed to go into the library, and they did not know how to get a library card.

> *"For example:* When you are "against" something, you are actually re-creating. You are creating more of the very thing that you want to eliminate! If you are "antiwar," think again. The operative word here is "war," and that is exactly what you will get more of. A better choice is to be "pro-peace." The universe will receive the vibration of "peace" and respond accordingly. The war on terrorism has created more terrorism. Violence attracts violence, and love attracts more love." (Jack Canfield, *KEY to Living the Law of Attraction: A Simple Guide to Creating the Life of Your Dreams,* Deerfield Beach,FL: Health Communications, Inc., 2007, pg. 32.

StarShine's philosophy and guiding principles include positive messages and almost no "anti-" curriculum or philosophies. Whenever possible, StarShine Academy chooses to form positive, forward movement and vision, rather than spend time on "anti-" training, i.e. anti-bullying, anti-drugs, anti-pregnancy or punishment. It is with this philosophy that we believe that children should not be suspended or expelled from school in most cases, but rather helped to work through any negative behavior by working on projects or development that create resolutions or solutions to the very actions that may have caused their negative behavior.

One day, a year or so ago, two little ten-year-old girls started fighting on the playground. Mrs. Shoop and I had been on the grounds that day and saw them. We brought them into her office and I began to explain how they were not being "StarShine" and that other schools allowed that type of behavior but not ours. I asked Mrs. Shoop to give me a large rubber band, which made the little girls eyes look very worried. I said to them, "Well I don't know what I am going to do. Normally, we have to expel students for fighting or you can choose to do a very hard, almost impossible thing. Which one do you want?" They looked at one another and then me and one of them spoke up and said, "We'll take choice number two." I almost burst out laughing but had to hide it. It sounded like they had watched too many game shows. "Okay, I said, stick out your hands." I could tell they thought I was going to do something like pop them with the rubber band. But I slipped the large rubber band over their arms and told them they had to keep it on the rest of the day without it falling off...it was about three feet long. I told them they had to tell everyone they met something nice starting with the teacher who happened to come into our room. They both turned in unison and said "You look really nice today." These two little girls have now affectionately been called the "Rubber Band girls" as they seemed happy to walk out of the door. A few minutes later as Mrs. Shoop and I were having a hard time composing our laughter, we heard a knock on the door. The little girls were back with two more friends who also wanted a rubber band. So cute! Needless to say, the girls became best friends after that. They had to learn to appreciate one another. They decided to work on an assignment together and to share the lesson with their class, "together."

They formed a friendship with each other that they thought previously as impossible. It also taught the other kids that it would be better to avoid fighting than have to work with a perceived enemy to repair it.

Cory

Cory Zortman was a sixteen-year-old Caucasian boy with a beautiful smile, beautiful eyes – and a terrible temper due to an abusive upbringing. He was angry at everyone and took it out on students and teachers alike, disturbing his classrooms constantly.

We worked with him over and over again, encouraging him to get ahold of his emotions when his temper flared, to stand on one foot and breathe deeply to calm himself down rather than lashing out at everyone around him.

We have a hypothesis that these white, disenfranchised kids throughout our nation are some of the most violent. They seem to be more shutdown than others because they are so alone. In many cases, the abuse they have lived with has been worse and they have almost no other adult support from other family members or even gangs. The mass shootings almost always involve a violent white kid. Those of us working with StarShine believe this could possibly be one of our most serious United States security issues.

It rarely happens at StarShine, but in Cory's case the time finally came one Tuesday when we had to tell him that he wasn't allowed to come back to the school; he wouldn't take responsibility for himself, and we could no longer tolerate his constant disruptions of class. He begged and pleaded for us to reconsider, but we said no.

The following Saturday night, he went to a party, where he met Nora, another student at StarShine. She also had come from a truly horrible background and so sat very quietly in the back of her classrooms, keeping to herself as she worked on her schoolwork.

Cory started to talk to another girl at the party and was approached by the girl's boyfriend, who told him to back off from his girl. Cory's temper flared once more, and he said some rude things to the guy. The guy he was yelling at was a grown man, with an even worse temper than Cory. Faster than anyone could react, he violently stabbed Cory fatally, then jumped over the balcony to make his escape.

The policeman answering the dispatch call for help, just happened to be a friend who found great enjoyment in coming to StarShine and volunteering time with the kids. He was very familiar with StarShine and most of the students, having spent time on the campus on numerous occasions. At the moment of responding to the call, he did not know the kid was a StarShine boy or that it was Cory. Cory died in his arms. Upon realizing that the boy was a StarShine student, he called me to let me know what had happened. He told me that it felt like he lost part of his family and asked me how he should handle it with the kids at school. I told him that he should come and talk with them, as he had been the one present when Cory died and had heard his last words. The kids at StarShine liked and trusted him, and deserved to hear about what had happened to Cory.

So he came to StarShine and spoke with them for a while, answering their questions and guiding a conversation about where to go from there. Nora, who had never said much to anyone at the school, sat in the back of the room, sobbing with a few of her girlfriends. Noticing her, I walked back to ask her to come into my office. She asked if she could speak privately to me and to the policeman and she began to tell us her story, one of an upbringing more horrific than the detective or I had ever heard. She also shared that she had been in love with Cory. When she finished, both the officer and I were stunned, we could barely speak, almost unable to breathe. I felt sick that any child should have to grow up in the way she described, this way, in our great country, the United States of America! At times like this, I get so angry that we have, each one of us, allowed these innocent children to endure such inhumane treatment. When I looked at the officer I knew that he felt the exact same way. If StarShine had been able to keep Cory twenty-four hours a day, he probably would still be alive. And if Nora had anywhere else to go we would not have heard her explain the atrocities that she had endured her entire life.

We have a secret in the U.S. We are growing thousands of white kids just like Cory. These kids are the ones that commit crimes and do mass shootings. These are the ones who have been dragged from motel to motel, and state to state by parents who should not be parents, people who know how to have sex but not much else. They run from the law because they are afraid. They are uneducated and lack any kind of moral character. They store guns in their cars and do almost anything to survive. They don't trust or care for anyone else. And they have babies who grow up to be angry, unpopular, fearful kids.

I was trying to figure a way to steer the conversation toward anything that might pull the energy up. I asked her what she wanted to be when she grew up. She replied that she wanted to be a singer, someone famous. I said that if she wanted to be a real singer, she should show us. The StarShine kids are used to "Running through the door of opportunities," so this was nothing new.

She quietly sang a few notes with a small smile. This seemed astounding to me again considering that she'd never seemed confident at all and hardly spoke in class, yet she had just unloaded her awful life history. Shortly afterward, Nora, the policeman and I hugged each other and said, like we always do, "Tomorrow will be a better day." I was totally without any more energy, and I know the officer and Nora felt the same way.

After they left, I gathered my things and I began to, heavily, walk out of my office door. Another student, Manny, stopped me in the corridor to tell me that he had heard my question to Nora and that he also wanted to be a singer. I looked at him and felt sorry for myself. As much as I did not feel as if I had an ounce of energy left, I got enough of myself together and told Manny what I'd told Nora – if he wanted to sing, he should let me hear him now. I happened to have a little video recorder and told him that it would be his first recording so to do his very best.

What happened next was another beacon of StarShine light on an otherwise dark, dark, gloomy day. Manny, an oversized, African-

American sweet boy, took a deep breath, paused, looked right into my eyes and began to sing in a sweet and clear voice "This little light of mine, I'm gonna let it shine. This little light of mine, I'm gonna let it shine, let it shine, let it shine, let it shine…"

STARSHINE GUIDING PRINCIPLE #3.

We each do the best that we can on each day, depending on what we know, understand, and feel, according to Maslow's Hierarchy.

If someone is hungry, it is very hard to teach them math or anything else. Unbelievable as it seems, one in four children are hungry in America today when they go to bed. This is another example of why a math test alone in second grade does not necessarily explain whether or not the child happens to have a good teacher. Whether the child is learning at an adequate rate is sometimes difficult if not impossible for the child's teacher to control. Maslow's Hierarchy suggests that all of us move up and down a scale each day that allows us to be more or less ready to learn and accept ideas, depending on how our various levels of needs have been met.

It is a little-known fact that anyone will become mentally ill within two weeks of becoming homeless, essentially because of the lack of needs being met. This comes as a surprise to some people who believe that homeless or disadvantaged people are there because they should be there, having been born at the wrong time or the wrong place. The truth is that we are all very similar when it comes to having struggles and being able to adapt to life. If these struggles become too extreme, most of us begin to behave in a similar, nearly predictable way. People who have been in war, often exhibit symptoms of post-trauma syndrome that are very similar and predictable to one another.

One of our former teachers, Brenda Combs has become famous as a speaker and advocate of homeless women. She was once a drug addict, homeless woman and victim of rape, gunshots, stabbings and at the lowest point in 115 degree Phoenix sun, shoeless because someone stole her barely decent shoes. She started a foundation called "Finding My Shoes." She earned her doctorate degree from Grand Canyon University last year and was our graduation speaker this past year.

When children come from dysfunctional families they tend to be dysfunctional themselves; unable to behave in acceptable ways until they can be helped and taught to behave in a different way. As adults, growing up with problems that they have brought from childhood, a "victim" mentality begins to form, which will affect their future behavior. This is one reason abused children often become abusive adults, who abuse children. Behavior is learned. Genetics plays a role, but not as much of a role as previously thought, and as I mentioned, there are exciting scientific breakthroughs that are beginning to suggest that our thoughts can affect our DNA.

It no longer makes any sense in saying someone is born into the right place at the right time with the right family or the wrong family, as if we can put barriers between certain groups of people. The world has become so connected that every person potentially affects everyone else. Perhaps for the first time in history our survival depends on the survival of everyone else, and our quality of life reflects the quality of life of those around us. Sophisticated technology has made it possible for one person in a bad mood to affect huge groups of people.

In the United States today we have more prisons and prisoners than any other country and at any other time in our history. Although prison-management companies themselves are making money, economically and ethically we cannot continue to put people behind bars simply because we don't know what else to do with them. We must re-develop systems of teaching each other what it takes to build a society that works to sustain itself. According to the New York Times, April 23, 2008, "As we have reported previously for the first time in the country's history, a staggering 1 in 100 Americans are behind bars."

It is perhaps not surprising, then, that the United States, with its current population approaching 304 million people, also "leads the world in producing prisoners", 2.3 million of them and climbing.

The United States has less than 5 percent of the world's population, but it has almost a quarter of the world's prisoners, according to data maintained by the International Center for Prison Studies at King's College in London. It seems as if we have become a nation of rule makers and rule breakers rather than a nation of principally driven people representing the "American Dream."

Indeed, the United States leads the world in terms of numbers of prisoners, a reflection of a relatively recent and now entirely distinctive American approach to crime and punishment. Americans are locked up for crimes — from writing bad checks to using drugs — that would rarely result in prison sentences in other countries, and they are kept incarcerated far longer than prisoners in other nations. Criminologists and legal scholars in other industrialized nations say they are mystified and appalled by the number and length of American prison sentences.

China, which is four times more populous than the United States, comes in a distant second, with 1.6 million people in prison. That number excludes hundreds of thousands of people held in administrative detention, most of them in China's extrajudicial system of re-education through labor, which often singles out political activists who have not committed crimes.

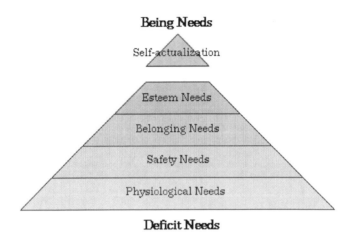

STARSHINE GUIDING PRINCIPLE #4.

Music is the first language.

Part of what causes the *"StarShine Effect"* is hearing music playing all over the campuses. When a visitor arrives, they notice chamber music playing. The music has a natural calming ability, which sometimes causes an emotional, often tearful, reaction. The main reason we play classical music is to increase the students' ability to learn.

All indigenous tribes use music to communicate, as do new mothers when they sing to their babies. In *This is Your Brain on Music: The Science of a Human Obsession* by Daniel J. Levitin, he describes compelling evidence that music prepares the brain to learn, and that early man first communicated through music. In his book (pg.226), he notes that "Glenn Schellenberg has pointed out the importance of distinguishing short-term from long-term effects of music. *The Mozart Effect* referred to immediate benefit but other research has revealed the long-term effects of musical activity. Music-listening enhances or changes certain neural circuits, including the density of dendrite connections in the primary auditory cortex." The Harvard neuroscientist Gottfried Schlaug has shown that the front portion of the corpus callosum - the mass of fibers connecting the two cerebral hemispheres - is significantly larger in musicians than in non-musicians, and particularly for musicians who began their training early. This reinforces the notion that musical operations become bilateral with increased training as musicians coordinate and recruit neural structures in both the left and right hemispheres.

There have been many studies of the brain and how it interprets information. We know that, just like fingerprints, every brain is unique and works in unique ways. Recent studies have resulted in findings that repudiate earlier research done on the brain, indicating commonalities in brain-function. For instance, it was widely assumed for many years that our brain cells do not change after the age of five. We know now that this is far from the truth. In fact, our brains change until our very last breath. Because our brains learn to repeat and facilitate repetition, habits are sometimes harder to change, but our brains can constantly re-wire and reproduce more brain cells.

Even today there are those individuals who dispute these findings. When the study called "*the Mozart Effect*" revealed that college student' scores improved on spatial temporal reasoning tests after listening to Mozart was first completed in 1993, it was widely criticized. Although Prof. Francis Rauscher and Dr. Gordon Shaw and many others continued their research and in the again in the late 90's provided another inspirational study that urged people on a national scale toward introducing classical music into children's education, many still would not believe it. In their study were two important notable conclusions:

- After receiving private piano keyboard lessons, Preschool children in Los Angeles performed 34% higher on tests for spatial-temporal reasoning than children who were either trained on computers or received no special training at all.

- After receiving a minimal amount of keyboard lessons students in two kindergarten classrooms in two schools in Wisconsin scored 36% higher on spatial-temporal reasoning tests than students who received no instruction.

Since at least the mid-1800s, research has found that classical music has numerous positive effects on children's development in education and health. (David J. Elliott, M.D., *Music Matters: A New Philosophy of Music Education.*)

In 1998, Georgia Governor Zell Miller founded an innovative program that resulted in the distribution of a recording of classical music, *"Build your Baby's Brain Through the Power of Music"* to all the babies born in Georgia between July 1998 and June 1999. The governor, Sony and tenor Michael Maguire picked the various selections on the recording, which includes works by Handel Mozart, Vivaldi and other composers.

"Rap to Roots" is the brainchild of Swallow Hill's music school director Michael Schenkelberg, who created it because public schools, particularly in the inner city, were losing their arts programs.

At the time he worked in Chicago and Cleveland, so he started the program in their public schools. Organizers tracked students' progress over four years and discovered that those in the program "did significantly better in standardized testing, attention spans in the classroom, and some improved their writing skills," *Denver Post*, 5.11.09

By combining multi-sensory learning, including music, evidence is compelling that proves that when children use music and rhythm to memorize facts like multiplication tables or the alphabet, their retention rate is three times higher than children memorizing without the music.

The Harp Foundation, one of StarShine's strategic partners, has done extensive research on how the Harp affects the muscles of the heart and brainwaves. Founding Director Joyce Buekers, formerly an IBM Executive, is a classically trained Harpist, carrying on a tradition from her grandmother, who was the Harpist for the Los Angeles City Philharmonic Orchestra.

For many years, Ms. Buekers donated her time to the transitional life organization, Hospice of the Valley. It was while playing for people who were transitioning from their human life and observing the patients during their last days that she began to be interested in studying the effect of the Harp on students who were in a learning environment.

We decided to bring as much Harp music as possible to the campuses both with live harps as well as recorded music and eventually bought small (Popsicle) harps to teach the students how to play them.

One of our board members, Sherry Lund, has led several health initiatives for integrated, holistic medicine. She opened Celebration Stem Cell Centre and introduced harp music with live harpists into many Phoenix area hospitals. The recent research that has been done on the healing effect of music, particularly harp music, should make all of us become more serious about the need to keep and grow music in our schools, businesses, homes and health care centers. Can you imagine what a difference it would make if families played music together even one night a week and turned off televisions and electronic devices?

In an article from MSNBC.com contributor Bill Briggs entitled, Music as medicine: Docs use tunes as treatment as researchers explore how melodies can help regulate heart and boost hormones, he quotes, "We're in the infancy," said Dr. Ali Rezai, director of the Center for Neurological Restoration at Ohio's Cleveland clinic. During a surgery called deep brain stimulation — performed while patients with Parkinson's disease are awake — Rezai and his team play classical compositions and measure the brain's response to those notes. "We know music can calm, influence creativity, can energize. That's great. But music's role in recovering from disease is being ever more appreciated."

STARSHINE GUIDING PRINCIPLE #5.

Beautiful, safe environments that are clean and include art, music and nature inspire creativity and help to secure man's sustainability.
"Earth is not a re-source. It is THE Source."
— Dakota Tribal Chief Arvol Looking Horse

On one of my recent trips, I had the privilege of visiting the corporate offices of Chick-fil-A. Mac Baker had invited me to tour their offices in Atlanta because he was very impressed by meeting some of our StarShine students when they were hired to work in one of the Chick-fil-A restaurants in Glendale, Arizona.

I take the time to observe environments carefully, comparing them with StarShine because I know that environments have such a profound effect on the productivity of the people contained within them.

The evident attention to detail on their property was one of the best examples that I have ever seen of a corporation supporting the people working there. The offices are a short distance from downtown, after taking a beautiful drive through wooded acres. The unobtrusive signage for the entrance is nestled among beautiful gardens and trees and as I drove up to the security guard, two men, dressed in beautiful suits greeted me with big smiles and a kind "Good morning! How can we help you?"

As I drove into the grounds, everything looked spectacular in the natural surroundings. At the end of a curved, gentle hill was the employee childcare center, a beautiful, renovated old Georgia mansion that had been restored to provide care to the children of the employees, near enough for the employees to visit with them when they feel the need. There are beautiful sculpture gardens throughout the property, along with gentle paths and lakes. "This," I thought, "is a creativity community."

As I walked into the front offices, two beautiful reception desks with fresh flowers in vases were on either side of the large hallway that looked like I was entering an enormous living room. A player-grand piano was playing beautiful music, and the fire was burning in the fireplace. Comfortable, beautiful furniture was coordinated with beautiful carpets and artwork. My impression was, "No wonder they have almost no employee turnover - no one wants to leave!"

They provide workout facilities and free restaurants for all of the employees. The restaurants are surrounded by huge windows, which made me feel as if I was in the middle of the forest on a dream picnic. I could feel the StarShine Effect there. People were smiling and seemed genuinely happy and pleasant. Everyone was helpful, no matter where I looked. People were greeting one another and constantly asking how they could assist me.

Notice how you feel as you read the description of the Chick-Fil-A grounds; can you imagine how the employees working there feel as they come to work? Contrast that feeling with walking into a typical school: Most schools look more like prisons than welcoming buildings as we walk up to them; many have huge fences, without any artistic appeal; few have music playing anywhere, as many schools have now reduced or eliminated their bands and choirs, not to mention their art classes. We have been so preoccupied with providing safety that we forgot the things that have the most profound effect on students' learning and achievement. Yes, we all need to feel safe and secure, but not at the expense of living in prison boxes that create the environment that we are trying to avoid. When was the last time that you saw a beautiful sculpture in a garden at a school? When was the last time that you walked into a classroom and noticed fresh flowers on the teacher's desk?

If we are to operate at our best, we need to constantly monitor the energy around us. What is giving us energy and what is taking it away? At StarShine we talk about things that suck energy, referring to people and yucky stuff. We try to help one another to notice what lifts us up and what pulls us down. Becoming laser-focused on creating beautiful, clean environments has one of the most profound effects on our daily output. If most of our attention is pulled in a direction that is off of what we intended, then we are not producing the results that we were trying to produce.

In order to produce the StarShine Effect, we look at the surrounding area and ask ourselves how it impacts body, mind, spirit, health, wealth and happiness. We do everything that we can to achieve the results that we want. We know that Baroque Music stimulates the brain and is pleasant to listen to, so you will hear Baroque Music many times at a StarShine Academy. We sometimes vary the music depending on what else we are doing, but the music is always pleasant and compelling as a background. There is a difference between "hearing" music and "listening" to music and both have profound effects on the human brain and growth.

The gardens at StarShine are part of the look and feel of the environment strategy as well as the learning that occurs there. In classrooms of StarShine certified teachers, children will experience gardening through small greenhouses and live plants growing in beautiful, natural pots. The teachers keep flowers on their desks. Many times the flowers on their desks are red roses, as they seem to have the strongest effect in uplifting most people.

You hopefully, will never see trash unkempt or dirty floors in a StarShine environment. Trash and messiness is one of the first things that will completely zap good energy or ideas. Keeping environments tidy, yet creative is one of the first things taught in StarShine, because disorganization causes a huge amount of frustration, lost time, and illness.

The children at StarShine formed a Picker Upper Club that is a very prestigious group to be involved in. Their purpose is to make sure that everyone remembers to pick up even the tiniest piece of trash and take care of it in the recycling bins or mulching piles. Our local Home Depot donated ten orange aprons and Picking forks for the elite club. The first president of the club was Carl, a first-grader who has to stay in a wheel chair. He has developed a pretty fancy way of using the picker upper and he chooses his club members very carefully.

As you walk up to enter the grounds of StarShine Academy, you will also be immersed in the beauty of art. Student art is displayed throughout the school. At the entrance, you will see our inspirational and valuable mural designed and donated by Vernon Swaback, a famous architect, author and StarShine board member. You will hear classical music and you will see sculpture and perhaps even bubbles from a bubble-making machine. You will read inspirational quotes. You will smell flowers growing. You will see children dressed in colorful clothes. You will experience a feeling of contentment and hopefulness from the moment you walk in. Music with art stimulates the brain toward becoming more receptive toward learning science and math, which produces creativity. Creativity emerges only from structure and balance.

Our environment is the world that we live in. We can no longer ignore the fact that we as a society are creating an unhealthy and, many times, very ugly world. We all have an individual responsibility to do our part in making it a better world - gardening, mulching, planting, recycling, refusing to use bleached paper due to the gases that are omitted – these are but a few ways in which we can make a huge difference together.

STARSHINE GUIDING PRINCIPLE #6.

Teaching and learning gardening is a necessary part of becoming one with nature and the environment and is a means for personal health and community building.

At StarShine, we use the garden as a metaphor for living and to teach and learn about nature, the environment, health and each other. The plants and vegetables in it are grown to teach about the environment in the world and the health of the students. Those plants nurtured the most grow strongest and taste the best.

There are a few organizations doing much to help the world heal by teaching communities to grow and use their local food, but we need more organizations, faster. Slow Food USA and Local Farmers Markets are two examples of wonderful, strong organizations, trying to make a difference. Trader Joe's and Whole Foods continually try to impact buyers to eat healthier. StarShine uses seeds that are certified organic from Seeds of Change in Santa Fe, New Mexico. Our sister garden in Sedona, founded by world renowned gardener, Adele Seronde, called Gardens for Humanity, is where we exchange many ideas for children's school gardening. In Australia, there is a huge movement by the government to include gardens and food preparation classes in schools.

Gardening is practically free, or at least inexpensive. But like everything it seems, we have over-complicated and massed-produced our food to the extent that we are all sick. We are a fat, sick nation eating processed, chemically enhanced junk that is not food at all, but stuff that makes us develop chemical dependency on the companies who irresponsibly produce the stuff. Marketing geniuses make us think it is good for us, but it isn't. The only thing good for us is the freshest foods we can obtain. Fresh foods have enzymes your body requires to have any energy at all. If you only eat fresh food, you won't be sick, or at least you will be healthier. Even today's iceberg lettuce is not really lettuce, it was "created" after World War II for mass production and is why your body cannot digest it. We drink pop and wonder why we can't lose weight. Pop is not a drink for the thirst in your body, pop and sugared or calorie-free drinks are chemicals that cause bodies to be sick. Our children trust their "adults" to feed them and teach them properly. But adults in the U.S. don't seem to understand the relationship to food, nutrition and being healthy. *"You are what you eat."*

The founder of Global Seed, and one of our sustainability expert advisors, Dr. Heather Devich, explains the necessity of replenishing the earth's soil by using decomposing garbage to create mulch. She says that with the rapid rate of losing good topsoil able to grow food, it makes it mandatory that every person on the planet with the ability to replenish the soil must do so, or we will, in our lifetime destroy the earths' soils nutrients that support growing our food. Can you imagine the impact on a company's culture if the break-room inspired everyone to make small mulching bins? Starbucks usually has leftover, used grounds that they will give to anyone for gardening, if you ask.

During the past fifty years, the use of chemicals on our crops and in our dirt has severely affected the quality of the nutrients as well as poisons in our food. At StarShine, we feel that the only way to build responsibility and appreciation for the earth's ability to produce appropriate soil and food is to require that every child work on gardening, growing, preparing and serving food, every day. What we did not anticipate about the school garden, until much later as we observed it, was the intense healing that seemed to be taking place within the spirit of our students.

St. Francis

I am not Catholic but I revere many things about the Catholic Church, including some of their saints, like Saint Francis. Saint Francis was born to a wealthy family and after several mystical events, decided to leave his family and his wealth to devote his life in poverty to preaching to common people. He did this without licensing or permission from anyone but with one simple rule for his lesser brothers; "To follow the teachings of our Lord Jesus Christ and to walk in his footsteps." And so he practiced being loving to all living things for his entire life.

He formed the Franciscan Order of Brotherhood who still today reach out to the poor without regard to their religious beliefs. It has been argued that no other man has ever carried his life so like the life of Christ. Stories surround Saint Francis and his ability to attract animals and birds. On at least one occasion he asked his followers to leave him alone so that he could preach to his sisters; the birds. There is another story about Saint Francis taming a wolf and making an agreement with the town dogs not to bother the wolf. It is told that the wolf laid down at Saint Francis's feet. According to Wikipedia, "He preached to man and beast the universal ability and duty of all creatures to praise God and the duty of men to protect and enjoy nature as both the stewards of God's creation and as creatures ourselves. Legend has it that on his deathbed, St. Francis thanked his donkey for carrying and helping him throughout his life, and his donkey wept."

Saint Francis's stories inspired me even as a young girl, having been introduced to his legends by my young Catholic girlfriend while living in Japan. His prayer, though most likely not written by him, is one of the most common prayers in the world used by Christians and non-Christians alike and is a guide for many of us who work with StarShine Schools and our gardens, as you will find the prayer etched in stone somewhere and placed in our garden:

Lord, make me an instrument of your peace.
Where there is hatred, let me sow love.
Where there is injury, pardon.
Where there is doubt, faith.
Where there is despair, hope.
Where there is darkness, light.
Where there is sadness, joy.
O Divine Master,
grant that I may not so much seek to be consoled, as to console;
to be understood, as to understand;
to be loved, as to love.
For it is in giving that we receive.
It is in pardoning that we are pardoned,
and it is in dying that we are born to Eternal Life. Amen.

I have had some coincidences several times involving St. Francis. One dramatic incident for me and somehow connected to the school happened many years ago now. It was on a day that I was feeling pretty low thinking about my daughter so far away attending school in the Czech Republic. I was thinking about her as I was driving down a busy street in downtown Phoenix when I noticed a sculpture garden on the side of the road; a little oasis. I felt like I should stop and take a walk through the beautiful sculptures, to try to get my mind in a better place.

As I walked through the quiet gardens, I felt a certain calming that helped me in my sadness. From the back of the garden, a small Hispanic man approached me and asked me if I was alright. I explained to him that I was missing my daughter. He told me that he had just finished carving Saint Francis and knew it was supposed to be for me, to give me comfort. He asked if I would walk over to look at it. It was a beautiful, three-foot statue of Saint Francis, carved from a particular stone known well in Mexico for gracing some of the most exquisite homes. Thinking it was an extravagance I could no longer afford because I was spending so much money to keep Courtney in school, I declined politely, explaining that I admired the statue but would not be able to buy it. The little man insisted, saying it had to be mine and he would sell it for only one hundred dollars. Carvings such as this one, even in Mexico are usually several hundred if not thousands of dollars, so I knew he truly wanted me to have this carving.

He picked up this very heavy statue of Saint Francis, about one-half his size, and he put it in the back trunk of my car. As I drove away, I was almost incoherent as my head was deeply thinking about Saint Francis and my daughter; I turned a corner in a quiet neighborhood where I had never been, just to try to relax. I drove a short distance and happened to drive up to a small Catholic Retreat center which I had never seen before, nor did I know it was there. I stopped my car to look at the little garden in the front of the church. I sat there, marveling at what seemed to me to be a lineup of miracles, as I noticed a man walking out of the front of the church toward my car. He asked if he could help me. I explained what had just happened and how I got there. He said, "This is a miracle, I am the priest here and I must bless your statue." Wanting to accept his kindness, I got out of the car and opened my trunk and right then and there, this little priest began a long prayer and blessing for my Saint Francis statue, my daughter and for me. As I drove away, I knew this statue was indeed meant for me and for some greater purpose.

A few days later, I saw Dr. Heather Devich who was working on our school garden. She brought into the garden an old bench and an old wooden spool, used to store large wires. She explained to me that she grew up on a farm without much money but with complete abundance. She said both of her parents used to sit on this bench every evening and spend time with each other and the family. She said her grandfather used the old wooden spool as a table and that she would sit on his lap for hours next to that table, listening to his stories.

One well-meaning volunteer with a group of boy scouts came a few days later to help work in the garden. She was helping to mentor our students in the garden and noticed the worn-out furniture that had been donated by Heather. She was bothered that we had "junk" in our brand new garden and asked me if she could have our students throw away the bench and the spool table.

I got a great idea. to explain to our students and to this volunteer about how sometimes the outside of what something looks like does not contain the preciousness of the story on the inside. I asked our students if any of them had a precious story on their inside that hardly anyone knew. They each acknowledged to me that they did have such a story. I told them that the only way others would be able to know them is through their stories and that they must tell them or they would be hidden, just like when they thought the bench and table were only junk.

The next morning I walked out to the garden and watched Heather as she surprised me with another gift and placed in the middle of the new garden more of her family's heirlooms; a small statue of Saint Francis along with a flat stone carved to display the Prayer of Saint Francis. Another synergy. For yet another time, I began to cry. Another StarShine Effect. I knew that our vision for StarShine was not our own; that it came from many before us and would be protected for many beyond us.

Dr. Heather Devich

Lizzie had never had a new blouse.

We were scrambling to get some new clothes together for Lizzie because she was about to go on her first plane ride. My mother had sent money to me to take Lizzie shopping! We had learned just days before that she had won the opportunity to fly to Kansas to speak to the Range Management Association about Ethnobotany and how the "StarShine Mustard Seed Garden" had helped her to experience her "Inner Self" for the first time.

When Lizzie first came to StarShine she was a very sad, withdrawn young lady, about thirteen years old. She had witnessed too much for a child or for anyone, and had struggled in school without many friends or support. She only wore black. When we went to the store, she told me she had never had a new blouse. She saw a turquoise one that seemed to take her breath away and I asked her if she wanted to try it on. When she came out to show me what the blouse looked like on her, I asked if I could take her picture as she seemed to have a glow, more radiantly than I had seen. That picture will be a memory I will never forget as it was the first time I saw Lizzie smile.

In her speech, she said that she had found her spirit in the garden, connected as she worked with the plants, and that she had felt peaceful for the first time in her life. This experience had created an urgency in

Lizzie to learn more, and she was led to discover "ethnobotany", which became a fascinating theme around the school. Lizzie would talk constantly to the other students about her discoveries on the subject. She said that cultures throughout history were defined by the many ways they used plants, not only to eat but to make useful things, ward off bad spirits, create medicinal remedies and art.

STARSHINE GUIDING PRINCIPLE #7.

Celebrating local culture and global diversity allows for a rich life.

We had to move a lot when I was growing up, as I was the daughter of a career Air Force Chief Master Sergeant. I was born in Frankfurt, Germany. I have always been very proud that as my birthplace I was among hardworking, people loving people, always focused toward trying to do their very best.

When we were living in Tokyo, Japan, I was complaining about having to move so much. My mom was talking to me about how important it was to create friendships with people that don't look like me. She said, "Trish, your life will be a whole lot more interesting if you will always try to make friends with people who look nothing like you." This may have been one of the reasons that I really believed I could open a school full of families that I did not know much about. I was just willing to learn and grow along with them. I believe that we are all similar, carrying our culture and pre-conceived ideas into every moment and that if we try to understand one another, we learn more about ourselves and our world starts to open up.

Because my family had roots in Colorado, Texas, Virginia and Oklahoma, we were greatly influenced and honored by our association with American Native Tribes. Some of their teachings and beautiful ceremonial dances have had a profound effect on my desire to search out similar customs in other nations. I loved the beautiful Kimonos of Japan and traveling with my family to exotic festivals to observe the many Japanese traditions, some thousands of years old. The reverence to history and the respect for elder's teachings with examples in Japan as well as on the American Native tribal lands have been sorely missing in many parts of the United States and the way that we help our children to grow. Today, more and more families practice fewer and fewer traditions and celebrations, which I personally feel ashamed about for our country's children, who don't know what they are missing.

When we at StarShine, prepared to observe the memorial for the first year after the disasters of 9/11/01 and decided to create an eleven days of celebrating schedule, I wanted the focus to include cultural practices from other nations as well as our own. We contacted Sister-City organizations in Phoenix and various embassy offices to ask if they would be willing to bring dancers, musicians and speakers in to help us celebrate 11 Days of Peace & Sustainability for 9-11——-21. The community support and interest was so overwhelming that we had to enlist a volunteer organization to manage the many volunteers and schedules.

Our nation has used the word "Tolerance" in many documents that have been negotiated and signed to initiate peace resolutions of one kind or another. I feel that even though the spirit of trying to get along is the intent of the use of this word, to me it is not enough. We, at StarShine, decided not to use the word "Tolerance" and to replace it with "Reverence" whenever possible. "Tolerance" still depicts a sort of hostile, yet calm, attitude toward someone else's viewpoint. It does not suggest respect; rather it suggests an unyielding, haughty resilience. It still undermines a real and earnest hope of understanding and compassion for another's position. The longer I live, the more evidence I see that when we spend enough time getting to know someone else, their fears, limitations and possibilities, our hearts melt, and we become understanding, loving human beings, able to get past our own insecurities and judgments to truly "Stand in another's moccasins."

One of my friends, Jane Edmunds, always signs cards that she sends with "Celebrate Well and Often." I have always loved this thought and many times have used it myself on cards to others. Our lives and our children's lives must be to encourage one another toward a sense of thanksgiving and traditions of celebrations. It worries me today to see so many children busily into their text messaging and game playing, so much so that they don't develop a true physical, human connection with another person, other than the one on the other side of the computer. They are not taught to observe traditions that uphold them into their future. Perhaps we can "borrow" other traditions to teach our own children in our families and our schools.

Our students practice being an ambassador of the United States and another country for an entire year. They must learn customs, executive protocol, traditions, difficulties and prides of the country that they represent and they must give regular reports to the other StarShine students. When people come to visit StarShine from foreign countries, they are paired with their StarShine "Ambassador" student for touring and exchanges in learning.

I believe that this tradition of immersing our students in other countries' celebrations brings out a natural curiosity of wanting to become a part of the global family of human beings and to experience more, rather than to close in and protect only what they know.

"The Way I See It #298: Our prejudices arise from the fear of things we do not understand. If my generation has a single goal, it must be to promote education — education that advances us not only technologically, but also intuitively and emotionally. In today's fast-paced world, advancing has to mean more than scientific discovery; it is our responsibility to force ourselves beyond

our comfort zones and become knowledgeable about the people around us." Jessica Arden Ettinger, Starbucks customer and student at the University of Virginia.

I kept this cup. It just happened to be on the back of my Starbucks' paper coffee cup. I was having a very heavy day and decided to go off to Starbucks to be alone for a few minutes. It seemed like a message, a sign to keep going.

STARSHINE GUIDING PRINCIPLE #8. *Practice: Connect versus Convince; Exercise: Compassion versus Judgment, Love versus Fear.*

"The illiterate of the 21st century will not be those who cannot read and write, but those who cannot learn, unlearn, and relearn." Alvin Toffler

Most of us at StarShine think that this principle is the hardest one to work on. Our natural tendency is to try to "make" people accept our opinions in the quickest way possible, especially with our kids, because we can - we're bigger, at least until they become teenagers. With enough force or the right tactics we can always get our way, depending on how much force is used, but resentment grows from it and will eventually show up. As a human race, we have not been taught how to work with those who have a difference of opinion, let alone a different set of natural ability or of different habits. We have been quite adept at getting rid of and not tolerating those who are bothering us. Our society has been formed out of command and control from our leaders, whether in religions, politics, corporations or families. Up until recently, it seemed to work - we have given and taken orders and complied.

We are the result of at least three generations of bad parenting. Not "Bad Parents" they are just parents, doing the best that they know how to; they have not been taught how to do it right. Good parenting is not taught in schools and it is usually not taught at home. Religious organizations teach some things about how to be a good parent, but many are steeped in the organization's need to intermix the parent training with a huge amount of guilt, which ultimately does not work in learning.

Some of the best parenting classes for how to effectively raise children, in my opinion, are the puppy training classes given at PetsMart. They teach people not to yell at or hit their puppies and to gently reward them, but not too much. They teach dog owners to create security for their new puppies by doing the same things over and over and over and over and over again. They teach you to feed your pet carefully and not give them junk to eat. They teach you how to love your pet appropriately and to help them grow up to be a pet you want to keep. They teach you that if you are going to have a great dog, you must be willing to do very consistent, responsible things every day.

Most people think that it is enough to love their children, but it is not enough. Parenting takes a huge commitment to do really hard things. Telling a child they can only watch television for one hour a week puts a burden on you as a parent to make sure of it and help to entertain them a different way. Telling a child they can't go to a party that you don't feel good about takes you willing to engage your child doing something else more healthy. Children need strong guidelines to develop the self-discipline they need to become happy adults and it takes great strength and courage from parents to provide it. You probably agree that you know some parents who could use a puppy training class.

More than ever, we need to prepare the next generations to be creative, to learn from one another and to establish a life that will be worth living. And to develop a strong sense of self-discipline, almost non-existent in our society. Today's world is about expeditiously connecting, whether you use the examples of Starbuck's, Facebook or

Twitter. We all need to learn a lot more about how to love and to be a lovable person. Hate, fear, bully, control, it's just a frustrating way to live, and it ultimately does not work. The old days of command and control are gone.

Even in the 1960s, Buckminster Fuller traveled the nation speaking about how authoritarian controls had stopped working. He believed it would work better if we designed a world that brought out the most good, rather than work within a political system that tried in vain to shut out the "bad." He predicted that with the increased use of computers, people would refuse to be "told" what to do. If you have a few minutes, I would highly recommend that you search StarShine's YouTube site for some rare Buckminster Fuller interviews. They are amazing to listen to. The things that he predicted back in the 1950's are phenomenally true today. He said that we would be talking to one another over a television.

Why was the highest percentage graduation rate was in 1969, with a decline every year since? Now in freefall, dropouts have increased to around fifty percent or more now. The reason that you don't see that fifty-percent number is because many schools don't report dropouts unless they drop out past tenth grade, but large numbers of students leave before then, sometimes as early as the fifth grade.

Did students become disillusioned with society in 1969 and start to question authenticity or integrity? Did society quit taking care of and helping our children to learn, to grow them into whole human beings? I wrote in one of my journals, "Have we started to give up on our own children's' ability to be held accountable to high standards and to help them get there?"

Here are some interesting facts that together may have stimulated the beginnings of a paradigm shift around 1969, away from the "Command and Control of Convince and Fear" toward a vast interdependence of "Connect and Love." Authority was being questioned on every front.

- 1968 - Martin Luther King was killed - "I have a dream..."

- 1968 - Youths interrupted the Democratic Convention; the country feared that it was out of control.
- 1969 - Sex, Drugs, and Rock and Roll
- 1969 - Neil Armstrong, the first man to walk on the moon, said, "'One small step for man; one giant step for mankind' are words that will live forever in the hearts and souls of humanity."
- 1969 – In July, a *Newsweek* review article on <u>Hair</u>, the offbeat show at New York City's off-Broadway Public Theater, described it as "a symbol of the exuberance of American youth…"
- 1969 – August - Woodstock - True believers still call the three-day event the capstone of an era devoted to human advancement. Cynics say it was a fitting, ridiculous end to an era of naiveté. Then there are those who say it was just a hell of a party.

  The Woodstock Music and Art Fair in 1969 drew more than 450,000 people to a pasture in Sullivan County. For four days, the site became a countercultural mini-nation in which minds were open, drugs were all but legal and love was "free". The music began Friday afternoon at 5:07pm August 15 and continued until mid-morning Monday August 18. The festival closed the New York State Thruway and created one of the nation's worst traffic jams. It also inspired a slew of local and state laws to ensure that nothing like it would ever happen again. (Reprinted with permission from *The Times Herald-Record* and Mr. Tiber)
- 1969 - 250,000 protesters, mostly young, marched against the Vietnam War in Washington, DC.
- 1969 – Dr. Timothy Leary presented his Berkeley lecture series "Visions of the Erotic Life", "How to Tune In, How to Drop Out" "The Counter Culture Consciousness<u>"</u>
- 1969 – November - American Indians seized Alcatraz Island in San Francisco.

- 1970 - The first Earth Day
- 1970 – May - National Guard opened fire on 1000 Kent State students demonstrating against the Vietnam War.
- 1970- The EPA was born; within five years it would be spending $2 Million per day.
- 1970 – Simon & Garfunkle produce their number-one song "Bridge Over Troubled Water".
- The 1980s became the Me! Me! Me! generation of status-seekers, mostly made up of Baby Boomers who gave up on their ideals and didn't believe in much of anything anymore, especially respect.
- The work ethic of new entrants into the labor market was under assault. *The "Entitlement Generation" - those born between 1979 and 1994 - have been described as impatient, self-serving, disloyal, unable to delay gratification - in short, feeling that they were entitled to everything without working for it. Not only were employees not concentrating as much on their work, they were less passionate, less likely to keep their word, less empathetic toward others and less likely to offer social support to colleagues. In groups affected by "Entitlementitis", workers reported more tense relationships and even higher levels of workplace depression.* Author: Brian Amble
- 1990 - Public use of the Internet began.
- America's silver tsunami: Over the next two decades, nearly 80 million Americans will become eligible for Social Security benefits, if they're there, more than 10,000 per day.

We can look back on these beginnings of a great crack in American values, starting to show.

Alan

Alan was one of our toughest kids. He was 11 years old. He had a rough home life. We were pretty sure that his mom was a working prostitute and heavily into drugs. Alan would tell us stories of turning the television up very loud in the living room so that he could sleep on the couch as there was only one bedroom in the house. He terrorized the school and the other kids. He was rude, angry and mean to everyone. He yelled cusswords in the classroom.

We tried everything. We encouraged him to read to the kindergarteners to build his self-esteem, but that didn't work. We took him out to the garden for hours and days, but that didn't work. After trading him from classroom to classroom, every teacher and principal trying to deal with him, he arrived with the help of Ms. Shoop to my office one day. She said, "I know that you think there is always a way through, but we have given up on Alan. He acts terrible and I recommend that he find another school, or you can take him." With that, she closed the door behind Alan, as she left him looking at me.

Ms. Shoop was creative and strong in her ability to help most students. I knew that she had reached a low point if she was giving me this ultimatum.

Alan locked his eyes on me, jetted his chin forward and said "F.U., get me outta this school!" I was shocked, really. That came out of an eleven-year-old? I said to myself, "God, I need help here." And then a thought came to me: If I can get him to turn, he will have the same conviction toward being good - he will always be strong.

Alan had opened the door and begun to walk hurriedly down the hallway. I caught up to him and said that I was not going to give up. I told him that I was going to walk all over the school with him until he decided to sit and talk calmly with me, and that we were stuck together. I said that if he walked too fast, I would hold his hand and that I expected him to be respectful. Well, that didn't work very well because he kept yelling at me and using obscenities. I just kept walking next to him and kept quietly saying that we could walk a lot or a little, it was up to him. We walked around the school grounds for forty-five minutes, and then all of a sudden, he walked straight to my office, plopped down on the Salvation Army Couch and burst out crying. My heart was bursting for him. I sat quietly down and put my hand on his little back. "Alan,' I said, 'you are a special child. You have had a hard time growing up, but this school will help you. You are here to make the world a better place. We are going to work together toward this. Some day you will understand why your life is this hard. It isn't fair but it is what we have to work with, so we just need to get going, to turn your life into what you want instead of what you don't want. There are not going to be many people willing to put up with a lot of bad behavior in order to help you. I am here because I care, but I am stronger than a lot of people and I believe in you even more. But if you don't stop fighting me, I am not going to be able to help you either. You have already been able to get the entire school to want you out, so I suggest you decide that you want to be here and work with what you have that Is GOOD in your life and then we can, together, start to turn it around. Will you at least try to work with me? I want you here. I see how smart and sensitive you are. We can do this. Are you willing to at least try?" The little guy looked so vulnerable, but he got up the strength to shake his head, yes. I said, "Ok then, what do you LIKE to do?"

Alan said that he liked computer games. This surprised me because I knew that he didn't have any computer games at home and had probably not played many. So then I said, "Do you want to learn how to create the games?" Alan nodded his head. "Ok, Alan, I will make you a deal. No more talking out in class. No more cussing. Respect and kindness toward everyone for twenty days, the time it takes to make a new habit, and we will go to the computer game college on a field trip, just you and me."

I think that this was a divine moment, because he looked up and just seemed different. He said, "I will." And he did. From that day, now over a year ago, he has been nearly perfect. Not completely, as sometimes he still has a temper tantrum. But he now understands that to calm down he needs to breathe slowly, stand balancing on one foot to gain some control over his brain and his thoughts, and he puts a vision of his goal into his mind, and that is what he does.

Alan has changed his goal of what he wants to be when he grows up. Sometimes he wants to be a game designer and sometimes a professional wrestler. We don't care, because we know that Alan is going to be something special.

Our brains are amazing. They get programmed to expect more of whatever they have come to experience. In other words, our brains go after the experiences that our brains are used to. If we are brought up to believe that we are powerful and respectful, we exhibit that behavior, because our brains are wired to do this. This is problematic if we have come to expect limitations, fear and disappointment, because our brains will continue to seek out the same set of circumstances. We have all heard that "If we expect good, it will happen and if we expect bad, it will happen." But too many of us still don't believe it. There is growing scientific evidence that not only is it true, but mankind's future may depend on how fast we learn about, accept it and work with it.

In a comprehensive study by Risley & Hart in 1995, in lower-socioeconomic families, a child will have approximately 300,000 interactions with an adult by the time the child is three years old, 80% of them are of a negative encounter, including yelling, abuse, ridicule, and anger. In contrast, in mid to higher socioeconomic families, a child will encounter approximately one million interactions with an adult by the age of three years old, 80% of the interactions are positive, including, talking directly with the child, cooing, praising, helping, guiding and encouraging.

A short time ago, researchers thought that the brain was formed almost to perfection by the time a child reached five years old. This led to the idea created by some experts to concentrate on the growth of very young children while making the assumption that if a child's brain was developed by experiencing too much tragedy or deceit, or if a child started their lives in violent ways, they would always exhibit negative behavior and it could not change.

This broad acceptance of inaccurate information has been a part of what has fed the "Victim" attitude that we have been taught to accept as normal. We know, and have proof that anyone can change at anytime. We intuitively believe in the possibility of any individual, given the right circumstances, to become a productive member of society. Yet, too many of us believe that if a child *did* do well after having experienced too many traumas, it was by divine decree instead of by a certain set of processes.

The ability to succeed comes from creating a burning desire for success within the individual. We are made to want to do things we want to do, not those forced upon us. This is how our brain is wired. Our brains will try to protect us from harm in all cases, including rules we don't understand or agree with.

Research is groundbreaking now, almost weekly, in the way the brain works and its amazing capacity to change until the day we cease our human existence. Every week there is more being discovered that completely changes the way we view the potential of a human being, at any age. It is exciting and frustrating at the same time. With all of the ability to research and collect data and use the Internet to communicate it, it seems that the most important stuff still does not get through so that we can use it to instantly improve our lives with it or the lives of our students in our K-12 schools. Filtering the most important, easiest to use information from the least important will become increasingly more critical as we continue to search for ways to create a sustainable future for living things.

IDC, http://www.idc.com a leading provider of technology analysis, reports that the amount of information transmitted globally over the Internet will continue to double each year for the next five years. That means that [in one year] the world will generate 57,000 times the total of all information in the Library of Congress. U.C. Berkeley estimates that global information increases about 30% per year. We are going to need a lot of help to decide which information we need to use. This will become increasingly important to what we teach in K-12 education. We simply cannot continue to teach the same things to our children and believe that they will be equipped to handle the changes that will continue to come in this expansion of information. Being able to easily adapt to change while having the ability to make deductable, sensible decisions is rarely taught to children in our schools and yet all of our futures will depend on quick-thinking, ethical decision making and leadership.

* Online information doubles every 6 months

* Corporate information doubles every 18 months

* Scientific information doubles every 5 years

* Biological information doubles every 5 years

* Useful genetic information doubles every 18-24 months

* The sum total of human knowledge doubles every 2-3 years (and is soon expected to double every year)

* Printed knowledge doubles every 8 years

* Technical knowledge doubles every 3 years

* Medical knowledge doubles every 7 years

* Each year around a million books are printed (that's titles, not copies), 25,276 newspapers are published (that is separate newspaper titles), 40,000 scholarly journals, 80,000 mass-market periodicals, 40,000 newsletters.

* Estimates based on the Netcraft Web server http://news.netcraft.com/ survey for January 2008 show there were over 155.5 million distinct websites, an increase of over 33 million from six months before. As of September 2011, the number of websites grew to 486,000,000.

As far back as 1995, Professor Peter Cochrane of the British Telecom Laboratories' Advanced Application Division said, "There are now wristwatches that wield more computing ability than some 1970s mainframes. Ordinary cars today have more 'intelligence' than the original lunar lander [Apollo Lunar Module]." In the decade since this statement, computer sciences and related disciplines have advanced exponentially.

Seventy percent of all information in our global society has been created since the start of the Internet.

Rates of depression have been doubling in some industrial countries roughly every 10 years. As of 2002, fifteen percent of Americans had a clinical anxiety disorder according to the Happy Planet Index Report http://www.happyplanetindex.org/ . The statistics expressed in 2002 are even more even gloomier now. In 2002 nearly 25 million Americans were prescribed and took antidepressants.

In 2003, U.S. doctors, resulting in $13 billion in sales, wrote 213 million prescriptions for antidepressants. Eli Lilly reports that more than 35 million people have consumed its breakthrough drug Prozac, the first in a new class of antidepressants, since it was introduced to the U.S. market in 1988. In the United States, the number of deaths from suicide over the past 20 years exceeded the number of deaths from AIDS.

Depression is now the fourth-leading cause of the global disease burden and the leading cause of disability worldwide. Depression seriously reduces the quality of life for individuals and their families and often worsens the outcome of other physical health problems. Depression is the most important risk factor for suicide (which claims around a million lives annually, with another 10-20 million attempting suicide each year), and is among the top three causes of death in young people ages 15 to 35. Statistics like these seem to be screaming at us to pay attention and look for a better way to live. Fifty years ago the average age for the onset of depression was over thirty-five, it is now down to sixteen!

The Department of Defense has recognized the importance of happiness in the military as having a tremendous impact on soldiers' abilities to perform their military duties. The Army, along with the University of Pennsylvania has launched the Army Resilience Training Center for Positive Psychology. According to Philadelphia Inquirer, Stacy Burling, writer, "Worried about rising suicide rates and thousands of soldiers with posttraumatic stress disorder, the Army is launching the Comprehensive Soldier Fitness program to help 1.1 million soldiers and their families cope more effectively with the stress of military life and combat."

The work of University of Pennsylvania psychologist, Martin Seligman caught the attention of the Army with his website, "Authentic Happiness, Introducing a New Theory of Well Being." It is a great website and offers many free questionnaires and worksheets for self-improvement and teacher resources for schools. His research and data proves the relationship between having skills of well-being and how that impacts skills of achievement. He has called out for Positive Education throughout America. "Positive education is defined as education for both traditional skills and for happiness. The high prevalence worldwide of depression among young people, the small rise in life satisfaction, and the synergy between learning and positive emotion all argue that the skills for happiness should be taught in school. There is substantial evidence from well controlled studies that skills that increase resilience, positive emotion, engagement and meaning can be taught to schoolchildren." From Positive education: Positive psychology and classroom interventions by Martin E.P. Seligman, Randal M. Ernst, Jane Gillham, Karen Reivich, and Mark Linkins

What good is a head full of knowledge if our hearts are empty and we lack peace of mind and purpose in life? What good are state mandated test scores if those scores are a only indicating certain knowledge but not a guarantee of a student's potential for success, ethics, happiness or determination? Are we such a simplistic nation that we only want to know whether a child is any good by the way the child scores on a math test? Perhaps the reason the child scores low is because he or she cannot read the test. Or perhaps the child is afraid of the test. Or maybe the child scored low because he or she was severely unhappy. And do we really, all of us, buy into the fact that if a teacher is not getting the kids to score high on prescribed achievement tests, the teacher is not any good? Really? What if the teacher spent the past two days with a child's family trying to help them understand how to support one another so that success can come to the child? The teachers whom have taught for StarShine are among the very best in the country. We make sure of it. And sometimes their students don't make high scores on the Arizona Achievement tests. But the teachers don't give up on the kids. And StarShine does not give up on the child reaching their potential. And StarShine does not get rid of great teachers because they don't get a particular test score from a particular child. We believe that every single child has the potential to become a great human being. But we know that some will never have a high math score, or a high science score. We at least, want the kids to grow up to be respectable, useful, hopeful, and happy citizens.

This is one of the main reasons that so many of us felt driven to organize an education system that took on more responsibility for the growth of an individual child, not only to gain knowledge but to gain compassion, understanding, happiness and an intense desire to improve oneself and the lives of others.

The 178-nation "UnHappy Planet Index" published by the New Economics Foundation, lists Costa Rica as the happiest nation on the planet. Meanwhile, Western nations with their high level of prosperity and abundance are way down the list. The UK and the U.S. fill 74th and 114th places respectively.[85]

STARSHINE GUIDING PRINCIPLE #9.

Individuals practice being ambassadors for their own country as well as a country other than their own.

StarShine students know that we each are each small part of a large world; the very air we breathe may have come from China and Japan. StarShine believes and teaches that the students must learn about their own value and responsibility in relation to others and the rest of the world. Each year the students, beginning in kindergarten, are assigned a country to study for the year and to figure out how to help that country's greatest needs. They act as the ambassador of that country for the entire year. If we have visitors from that country, which happens quite often, they are assigned to the ambassador student as their StarShine Academy tour guide.

We recently created a strategic partnership with Lift Up America http://www.liftupamerica.org/ to accredit and use their curriculum for our students and share it with other schools. They support StarShine's desire to instill American respect and citizenship back into our schools and student's lives. As the children focus on learning about veterans and their history, they begin to develop compassion and understanding for America's history and they begin to see their part in building it for future societies. The Joe Foss organization, http://www.joefoss.com helps veterans to connect to schools and mentor the students to help in bridging the relationship between school children and our country. StarShine teaches that true patriotism is one that is lived every day in our every day existence as we appreciate our forefathers who fought for our country but also always reached out to help others. It is sad that in most schools today almost nothing is taught about what it means to be an American citizen. Yet in every other country children are taught about America as the "The Land of Promise."

Diamond

Diamond is a darling little girl. She has more spunk than a sparkler on the Fourth of July. She is eight years old, and her country assignment for her ambassadorship this year is Iraq. On one visit, my sister Darlene Sibigtroth, one of our board members, was walking through the school grounds toward the StarShine garden. All of a sudden, this little girl came running across the playground and an excited little Diamond invaded Darlene. "Hi," Diamond said as she stuck her right hand out to shake Darlene's hand. (The kids all have to learn how to shake hands and introduce themselves.) "My name is Diamond and I am the Ambassador of Iraq. Have you heard about Iraq? Iraq is really right next to Iran." With this she used her two hands in front of her to show Darlene how close the two countries were. "Well," she said, "Those two countries are not getting along at all. They are fighting with each other." And with this she began to wiggle her fingers on both hands, like they were starting to create a commotion between each finger.

I just about lost it. I wanted to burst out laughing but did not want to divert the seriousness of Diamonds' explanation. This might not have been rocket science class, but what a very precious moment of learning, empowerment and compassion. This little girl had an understanding of two countries halfway around the world and was concerned that they needed to get along. Darlene talks about this story often. In one small moment, we cannot predict the ripple effect caused by a little girl, empowered toward leadership.

This kind of teaching is of primary importance to StarShine's curriculum, but how can we measure it? Would we downgrade Diamond's teacher if Diamond scored poorly on her math test? Doesn't it seem absolutely critical that we teach skills that we all need? StarShine teachers and students work hard at getting the students individually involved in their learning and their passions. Eventually it drives their spirit as well as their competition toward excellence. You can't "make" kids learn and you can't "make" teachers teach. Teachers and students must be given opportunities, expectations and the tools they need to reach excellence, otherwise our country will fail, just like other countries have in the past.

People say that America is too great to ever fail. That is what was told to me about AT&T when I worked there as a young executive before the court ordered the divestiture of AT&T. Overnight AT&T was broken and most people thought it would never happen.

America's children are screaming for help. American adults are a mess. American teachers are the most important people in the world and they need our support and our research, not more rules and compliance.

Learning about other countries is so natural at StarShine I sometimes forget how forward thinking this is compared to most other United States' schools. Some educators for "confusing our students with too much 'outside' information have ridiculed us. In countries in Europe, because they are all so close to one another, the students continually learn about other countries, including the United States. As I have traveled abroad, I am astounded at the facts that children from other countries know about their own country as well the United States. But our kids know very little about the U.S. and certainly not much of anything about other countries.

We provide situations for our students to actually experience customs and politics from other countries, because "doing" is a much more efficient learning method. The students learn more quickly and become impassioned in understanding and enjoyment of differences. We hope to one day establish a StarShine Peace Corp to assist in helping other schools or environmental projects in the world by bringing our high school students and StarShine Alumni into other countries. When funding and coordination becomes available, these two-week trips will become mandatory for all of our students beginning with the eighth grade. The Institute of EcoTourism, http://www.ioet.org has been working on development of this program with StarShine because we all believe that when any of us travel to other countries, we learn about how important one person is to all of society. Our students seem prepared to help other countries and to understand how important this is toward building a peaceful, productive planet. Worldwide Opportunities on Organic Farms http://www.wwoof.org is another great organization that helps place young adult global volunteers from around the world to work in organic gardens in all parts of the world (and at StarShine.) Our students, because they already are taught organic gardening are a perfect fit for the organization after they graduate from StarShine.

Recently we hosted visitors from the Tohono O'odham Native American Nation, considering establishing a StarShine Academy on their lands through working with Vernon Swaback and his architectural firm. One of our little girls, a nine-year old saw the group from across the playground and came running over to greet them. With her hand outstretched to shake theirs, she said "Are you from the reservation?" As I started to interrupt, not knowing where she was headed with this question and not wanting to cause our visitors any discomfort, one of them quickly answered that indeed, they were. The little girl added, "Me, too. I am part Hopi and part Navajo. Can I stay with you while you are here at our school?"

I never know what to expect at StarShine, hence the "StarShine Effect" and this was certainly no exception. I was so surprised at the sweetness of the moment. Amazing me, she went on to explain that she would like to be an ambassador for their nation. I said that since they were a sovereign nation, I thought that it made complete sense.

This request endeared the little girl to the Tohono O'odham Council Members, one of whom had barely seemed to be interested in the visit. A little while passed and this tribal leader all of a sudden spoke up and said that she had wondered why she put her "Dream Catcher" necklace on that morning, but now she knew. In a small ceremony, the leader presented her necklace to this excited little girl, whose eyes and I think her heart was forever changed, as the necklace was placed around her neck. Another member, the tribal chief, then walked over to say a blessing in his native language as he placed his hands on her head. Our entire group was stunned by this magical moment. Most of us were in tears watching this miracle unfold, another magic StarShine moment. I couldn't stop thinking about how education and knowledge doesn't get any better than this. Now how would we put this on an assessment test?

STARSHINE GUIDING PRINCIPLE #10.

Co-learning demonstrates that every person is a teacher and every teacher is a student.

It's what we don't know we don't know. The more we learn and the more we think we know, the more we realize we don't know. We only know what we know and we don't know what we don't know. At StarShine we require great teachers. But we look for teachers who are curious learners, not just experts in their fields, experts who can't wait to challenge their knowledge. Our teachers look at themselves as great coaches, great and always curious learners, and coaxing students into reaching further than they think is possible. They constantly raise the bar for themselves and for their students.

As I look back on my own education and my teachers, it wasn't always the nicest one that helped me the most. I do believe teachers should be kind no matter what, and we surely employ energized teachers at StarShine, whom we like to be around, but I also know that sometimes even grouchy teachers have been able to get children to accomplish break-through perceived limitations, when they have a passion for their craft, their courses, excellence and the kids' futures.

One of my own teachers in high school was a perfectionist. I am not sure that she was happy in her life. But I look back on the time that I was in her Honors English class and what I accomplished in that year. She truly believed in my ability and would not allow me to do anything less than what she thought was possible. And she thought she knew more about the English language and literature than anyone on the planet…and maybe she did. It may have been her constant displeasure with my writings, making me do them over until I got them right, that gave me the idea and courage that I could write. She was extremely hard to please. Earning a compliment from her was indeed an accomplishment. I still remember her fondly as one of my most impactful teachers. I don't remember her smiling, although I remember how fiercely she defended excellent English writing and speaking skills. And when I got an A, I thought I had done something incredible. Well, I had.

As we continue to research and develop our own StarShine Quintessential Institute for Teachers As Leaders Training, we have had much discussion on what makes a great teacher and how best to provide the training that the best teachers require. We know one thing; the single most important factor that leads to someone learning is that the teacher has a passion for what they are teaching. Does that make so much sense?

If you look at classrooms today in the United States, the passion has nearly been removed from the teachers. They are not free to teach with passion. They are told to get the test scores up and they are completely stressed out. They are told to teach subjects they don't even want to teach, so how can they be passionate? They are required to do too much exhaustive paperwork, leaving them less rested to work with the students, whom most of them love.

Of course there are many factors involved in identifying an outstanding teacher, but one of the most important factors is that they have the stamina to expect and carry through on raising a students' capacity to perform better than they thought they could. We all need coaches throughout our lives, to insist on developing our ability to do something that we think we cannot do, and to work with us until we indeed are able to. We all know the experience of telling a class to reach as high to the ceiling as they possibly can on their tiptoes, and then saying "Now reach higher." We all only achieve what we think we can. We need someone beside us inspiring, expecting more and encouraging, maybe even demanding, us to do it. We all expect so little. We can all do so much more, more effectively and do it better toward becoming happier.

STARSHINE PRINCIPLE #11.

Financial literacy fosters hope, belief and abundance as it facilitates a wise use of assets.

So why AREN'T kids taught financial literacy? Why do we have a nation of finance idiots? A long time ago, leaders in the United States got together to create what we now have in our education system.

Before StarShine, I was a banker for several years. Some of the most well known names in the community were my clients. I worked with national politicians who had many secrets, doctors who owned several clinics but lost a lot of money and lots of attorneys who wanted huge dollars for their hourly fee but could not pay their bills, so had poor credit ratings. I helped them to write business plans and to prepare for loans for houses, companies and jets. I helped to position them for venture funding.

I was constantly amazed at what they did not know about the most primary of financial rules, like don't spend more than you have, and buying "stuff" doesn't necessarily buy happiness, or just how to decide whether or not something was an asset. Time and time again, my clients would arrive in my office looking like they were on the edge of a breakdown. Many of them were.

One client of considerable wealth and dignity, and known for his ethical behavior, came in one day to refinance his mortgage to get a lower rate. He brought his new wife with him to introduce the two of us. I had known him for years, and he never carried much debt. He had two credit cards and they were always paid off each month. As we all sat around my desk, his credit report started printing pages and pages of credit accounts. I was trying to remain unconcerned but became very aware of the way his eyes focused on the pages that were printing. His new wife was looking at the floor, acting as if she wanted to be somewhere else. When I assembled all of the pages for his review, he became outraged. "Trish, these are not my accounts! You know that I don't use this many credit cards!" His wife, in a rather meek tone said, "They are ours." My poor wealthy client had been blindsided by his own wife - she had charged close to $100,000 dollars worth of "stuff" on cards that were in both their names. He sat there motionless, with a chalky-grey face. I felt so sorry for him, and for her. For him, he had been duped by his own wife; for her, because she had so many insecurities that drove her to this behavior.

I used to say that I felt very humbled to know so much about the families I had as customers. They would have rather gone to the dentist naked than have to explain to me their financial situations. Unfortunately, time and time again, I had to work through the devastating finances caused by divorces that were caused by couples unwilling to be completely honest with their spouses about their spending and saving. Fear drives a lot of bad decisions and eventually costs money, marriages, families and countries.

When I was in banking, I volunteered to help the community learn empowerment tactics in dealing with money. I gave lectures and taught in adult and high school classrooms about how to manage money and credit. I wrote various pamphlets and designed short courses for others to teach.

It is not about how much you have, but rather your relationship to money and other people that define you. Money itself has no power, it is the *use* of money that creates or diminishes power.

The main difference between rich and poor is in the terminology that is used with regard to money. A popular, sadly true saying is that poor people live for Saturday night and rich people live for seven generations. Poor people tell their kids that they will never have any money and rich people talk about how well their investments are doing and what responsibility their children have in taking care of it. How you think about something determines your future.

As a part of my mortgage investment company's community outreach, we scheduled a public relations event that led me to meet Robert and Kim Kiyosaki of *Rich Dad Poor Dad* *http://www.richdad.com* and *http://www.richkidsmartkid.com* . I did not know that they lived in Phoenix. I reached out to them before many people were aware of their work and asked them to facilitate one of their Rich Dad *Cashflow* games for a group of well-known people in the financial industries. I wanted to broadcast a radio and television show observing several live games of financial gurus playing the game while Robert and Kim made comments as a public relations event.

The night of the broadcast we had a lot of fun, leading to a life-long friendship and partnership, but the discussions we had that night regarding the lack of financial accountability of the public became very serious. As a community outreach, my bank focused on teaching entrepreneurism and financial accountability to the youngest of children, unusual then and now.

Without understanding how to ethically and morally "use" money instead of people, we are doomed as a nation. Without teaching the poor how to "make" their own financial dreams come true, we will become a nation of high taxes and low morale. People must feel significant to live a life that can be fulfilled. They must be given tools that enable them to make strong, wise and prudent decisions. Giving people money and attaching no or too little responsibility or self-discipline to it, only leads to unhappiness and unproductively. In fact, in the book *Predictably Irrational* by Dan Ariely some very interesting experiments and conclusions were made linking money used for incentives actually causing the opposite, poorer results. Many parenting groups have used this warning: Do not pay your kids an allowance for jobs they should do just because they are in the family. Things like bed-making, homework, setting the table should be done as a part of the responsibility to be a part of the family and not for money! People do not realize how money can actually cause damage to a person's willingness to do their best.

When I decided to open the first StarShine Academy, *Rich Dad* Kim and Robert Kiyosaki and one of their partners, generously wanted to support me (and challenge me) and my dream to make a difference, and they donated the first $25,000 for me to begin the school. They also donated *Cashflow* games and many books, both in Spanish and English. We had parent seminars to teach and give out the books. I remember vividly the first parent coming to me with tears in their eyes. Not only had it been the first book that they ever owned, they told me it was the first time they started to understand that they were allowed to have their own bank account.

In America, the land of opportunity, we have overlooked for too long, the importance of how our country was founded and what made it become the beacon of liberty and freedom throughout the world to gain financial freedom. Our forefathers knew how to begin a nation that could work better financially, out from under strict control. They knew what was wrong in their previous country and they wanted to begin a new form of government and opportunity that welcomed good ethical decisions and business practices. It was this amazing pioneering spirit that brought the United States to continually evolve to be known for being able to figure out better ways of doing things.

We constantly hear about how well Chinese students perform in math, but what they do not understand is how to think critically or how to motivate others or how to solve problems or to become entrepreneurs. And they want to know these things. In nearly every conversation with Chinese education dignitaries, "How to teach students how to become entrepreneurs, not how to better memorize math" was the foremost question.

No matter where I travel, people want to come to the United States and they believe it is the ultimate place of freedom and inspiration. They get a look in their eyes as if they see in their mind's eye, a castle on the hill, beckoning everyone with a bright light of hope, intense abundance and beauty. I think they see a picture of Disneyland for everyone who comes to the United States.

STARSHINE GUIDING PRINCIPLE #12.

Partnering and mentoring fosters interdependence toward building common ground, as in: "the world agrees on time so everyone can communicate".

Developing life-long strategic partnerships is a foundational basis of StarShine, and it begins with the students helping each other, outside businesses mentoring students and parents fixing school grounds. Partners for our technology use StarShine to test processes, and we in turn get to have the most cutting-edge technology for a discounted price. We are very careful about choosing our business partners. We try to always be with those "best in class" so they are encouraged to help one another by cross selling to each other's customers when it makes sense. We encourage win/win partnerships in every process, causing StarShine to continually improve because the individuals involved continue to self-improve.

Our once famous relationship with Toshiba began completely through one wonderful person, Gene Udvare, dropping by the school to sell a copy machine. We couldn't afford one, but we always treat everyone like a much-anticipated guest and on that first day, that is what Gene experienced. Dory Rockcastle at the front reception desk, always a friendly face, treated Gene with as much appreciation as if he had donated a copier, let alone tried to sell one. He began to drop by the school whenever he was having a bad day. He said that the kids made him feel like they cared about him. Then one day about three years later, he decided to take some of our students to one of the biggest of PGA Golf tournaments, the Waste Management Phoenix Open. He wanted to inspire the kids and show them how they might be able to enjoy their lives one day if they work hard. He bought bright red long-sleeved, tee shirts for them with the name TOSHIBA in big letters down one arm and STARSHINE ACADEMY down the other.

Our own KidStar, Young Reporters, ESTR Radio Show students wanted to interview some of the golfers at the tournament, so we practiced the night before. I asked the kids if they could pick their very favorite golfer to interview, who would it be? None of us knew who the golfers were for the tournament, we were just pretending. Most of our kids are Latino, so they almost unanimously said they would love to meet and interview the famous Latino television star named George Lopez. Ok, I said, I will pretend to be George Lopez and you have to interview me. So for a few hours that is what we did that evening. They would ask George questions with their fake microphone in hand and I would pretend to be him answering them.

Always for the kids radio show, the students practice what they might say if they meet someone famous. And as God has so many times smiled on StarShine, the first person they saw coming down the fairway around 8:00 a.m. was, believe it or not, George Lopez! Amazing! And boy, were they ever ready! I thought they were going to attack him! One of the smallest kids seemed to holler the loudest to ask if he could interview Mr. Lopez. They were prepared to meet opportunity. Sure enough, George Lopez walked right over to our group of red-shirted Toshiba-StarShine sleeved kids and they started firing the questions as we videotaped. Television cameras came running, wanting to know who these kids were. They certainly did not seem to be kids from a tough neighborhood. They got tons of attention and Toshiba got a huge amount of free international advertising. Mr. Lopez seemed to enjoy the kids, maybe because there weren't many others kids around, maybe because they were mostly Hispanic, or maybe because they had their act together. As they talked every television camera kept rolling to get all of this on international television. That is what happens to StarShine kids. They earn it.

Creating inter-dependent relationships of win/win of support, accountability and inspiration is an easier way to live. The world is too complex to try to do it alone or by launching a huge marketing campaign or worse yet, a war. It is less expensive, more effective and more fun to do things together and try to help each other in fun, reach heights never tried before. This is the beauty inside of a great marriage, a family or a huge corporation and should be taught in every school.

STARSHINE PRINCIPLE #13.

Holistic explains that each event reinforces all. The pursuit of success and happiness, both individually and collectively, must include body, mind, spirit, health and wealth.

This is a story of everything going wrong and everything going right. It's always about the whole thing.

A few years back, well actually, it has happened more than once, we experienced a pretty bleak time. We were asked and had decided to open a new school site in another under-utilized Episcopal Church property in the northwest part of Phoenix. It was summer in Phoenix again, with more record heat than the previous year. Jan and I organized a new/old staff outing to hand out door hangers to announce the new school opening, in hopes of enrolling new students in the neighborhood. As we divided the streets and door cards, we began to walk the streets in twos. For a while Jan and I walked together, and I noticed that her cheeks were getting really bright red. I questioned her about it, and she said that she was hot but wanted to finish putting up the door hangers.

Meanwhile, we had just opened StarShine Academy school number one for another year and were in the midst of training the new teachers as we were getting ready to open the second one. The new first-grade teacher, Crystal Mosca, now our registrar, was very excited and had been working with Dan Ciskal, our wonderful kindergarten teacher, who is a cross between Captain Kangaroo and Mr. Rogers. They had computers and papers all organized and ready to go in neat stacks on their floors.

Over the weekend, the pipes in the water heater burst and flooded our kindergarten and first-grade classrooms, ruining everything. The safety inspector said that we could not have kids around the building because they might breathe in mold. So we had to relocate the classes to the already-crowded cafeteria-great room. Then that evening I got a strange message from Jan saying that a small cut in her elbow from the day was getting really swollen and that she did not feel well.

Jan's husband, Steve, called me the next morning and shocked me with the news that the doctors at the hospital were trying to save Jan's arm! She had contracted some form of staph-strep that was spreading so fast that her life was in danger. I could hardly believe my ears let alone my heart. And once again, I began to cry. What in the world was I going to do? I didn't even know where things were kept. We had all been so busy that we didn't have the energy or the time to get cross-trained. As for Jan, I knew that her resistance had been compromised when we were in that heat, and I felt horrible that I had not stopped her.

Everything was a big mess. We were going minute-by-minute, using as many volunteers as possible, trying to keep both schools running as smoothly as possible. But it seemed like this was not enough.

A couple of days later, I was at a mandatory meeting out of town when I received the next phone call. The gardeners had accidentally disturbed a huge hidden wasp nest, and the wasps were swarming the school. The fire department was on their way, but in the meantime, some of the StarShine workers had been lighting towels on fire and giving them to the kids to whack the bees, because they understood that the bees wouldn't like the fire and smoke and would go away. This plan backfired when the bees started to sting the kids and some of the adults.

As I stood there with the phone to my ear, listening to all of the commotion and background noise, being so far away, picturing the kids running around with burning towels, I thought for a minute that I would faint, and then I became very peaceful, almost numb. All I could think about was a verse in the Bible, 2 Chronicles 20:9: "Should evil come upon us, the sword, or judgment, or pestilence, or famine, we will stand before this house and before You (for Your name is in this house) and cry to You in our distress, and You will hear and deliver us." I could do nothing to help at that moment but pray.

And we were delivered. All of the teachers pitched in, some thinking better than others, and some of the kids acted like true heroes. The firemen did their work, and we were just barely mentioned in the press. Thank you, God.

In the meantime, Jan was being fed massive amounts of drugs and antibiotics and was responding favorably to the surgeries and doctor's care. We weren't allowed to talk to her, but her husband kept us informed. One by one little miracles kept happening that fixed things and provided moments of peace. I could write an entire book just on this one StarShine moment and what we learned, as there were so many people and magical solutions that came forward to give the schools the support that they needed and that I needed.

We talk a lot about how the word "holistic" means body, mind, spirit, health, wealth and happiness for an individual, but it also predicts how we bring our entire selves into the connection with the community and with the rest of the world.

Think about Google and the way it collects information as well as gives it. In keeping with Maslow's Hierarchy of the Theory of Motivation, StarShine believes that we bring to each moment all parts of our body, mind, spirit, health, wealth and happiness. If a child is hungry, he or she will not be learning until they get something to eat. And if a child comes into the classroom worried about her parent, the child will not have her mind on learning.

We separate health from our bodies' and minds' choices of food, behavior, and exercise. We put kids in rows of desks and chairs separate from what we know about how the brain works. We separate the dirty air we breathe from the car we want to drive. We separate our spouse's happiness from our own. We separate our own choices from the outcome that we live. Everything affects everything else, including our intention in the first place. If we look at everything trying to find wrong, we will. If we look at everything trying to find right, we will.

I am frequently asked to present a lecture I call, "Growing Your Global Brain." It is in part about Internet usage, but it is also a metaphor that incorporates how we let our own brain operate and how we are all collectively influencing all of our behaviors all of the time, depending upon our small choices while continually influencing the Internet. The audience typically asks me the question "Can we in schools teach our children to become ethical, inspired citizens who will figure out and participate in solving their own problems?" To which I always respond the same way: "We *must* do this. Schools are the one place where all of the children and families are gathered in a hopeful place. Most children are not learning what they need from the adults in their lives. Many customs that previously taught ethical behavior are not being practiced by families and taught to the children."

StarShine incorporates a thematic approach to education layering curriculum, themes and principled living throughout every lesson to include body, mind, spirit, health, wealth and happiness all of the time. We teach the way our life actually works, all together, not in neat rows or in small dices of themed times, but in everything working together. We continually research for the most basic things that drive human behavior and ethics and drive passion and kindness and we use it in our classrooms. We are still public schools so we must apply the required standards as well as national and international standards. I agree with standards in most cases, but only as a beginning focus for education so that we all have a form of agreement. But the standards should be used only as a guide for what we want for our children, certainly not the only things they need to know. And we should use them as guides

234

because many of our most talented children will never be able to meet all of the standards.

The crisis we are experiencing in banking, health care, the environment, our food production and in education are partly due to a too truncated approach to problem solving. In order to reach great solutions to anything or to create amazing breakthroughs, all things must be considered in a holistic, interactive way and put into an organized system of pro-action.

STARSHINE GUIDING PRINCIPLE #14.

Leveraging technology facilitates connecting people; personal contact is vital.

The only way that we can grow StarShine's presence in an expeditious way is to leverage technology. And the only way to deliver customized student instruction is by using technology to reduce costs.

Although word of mouth advertising is still the quickest marketing tool, Twitter or Facebook might be a close second. Technology helps in many ways; but it is diminishing personal human relationships. Obviously technology has made it possible to find appropriate dates or friends, but it is also destroying social skills that build long-term relationships and happiness we all need.

Appropriate technology is as important a topic as integrity and trust. I love using technology and it is connecting us in a way that makes so much possible that was previously not. But where "Two or more are gathered, all things are possible." We need one another, as close as we can get it. Developing relationships, a personal community that supports one another is of paramount importance, especially in person. We have seen the pictures of soldiers at war, holding children from villages in their arms and have been moved to tears. This closeness is the thing we all need.

MasterMind

I read about MasterMind Groups when I was in my twenties. My mom had bought for me and always influenced my reading of Norman Vincent Peales' *Positive Thinking* and Napolean Hill's *Think and Grow Rich* and she bought my first subscription to the *Science of Mind* magazine when I was eighteen years old. So I learned at an early age that thoughts are things. "What you think about you bring about. Believe it and you will see it and achieve it. Whatsoever the mind can conceive and believe, you will achieve. If you think you can or you think you can't you are right. The universe supports those with great focus." I memorized prayers of empowerment and I learned to meditate, pray and quiet my mind. I learned to make visualization mindmaps and experienced their power. And I wanted to join a MasterMind Group.

There is evidence of MasterMind Groups throughout hundreds of years of history; people coming together, mostly in person, to support one another's ideas, visions or goals in a trusted group, meeting at a regular interval. *Master Keys System* by Charles Haanel was written to explain the power of thought in the early 1900's but was banned and taken from the shelves because it was too controversial. *As A Man Thinketh* by James Allen was written in 1903 and yet I doubt any K-12 school today teaches with it.

I met my girlfriend, Joy Jacobs Bancroft when I first moved to Phoenix in the late 1980s and within minutes of meeting her, she suggested I join her MasterMind group, led by Rev. Merilyn Chilleen. I had written in my goals many months before, that I needed to find and join a MasterMind Group. We both knew it was fate. Over the years, the prayers answered, were seemingly miracles after miracles. Later, Mia Martori, StarShine's current board member and I formed an offshoot of the original MasterMind group and met with one another every other week. It was Mia and I that formed two charities, one was StarShine Academy with a garden in it, and one, The Institute of EcoTourism, to help promote a sustainable way to impact the environment through travel. Both were the outcome of prayer and our MasterMind Groups.

Please see the Appendix in the back for web links to free instructions for forming your own MasterMind Group and in joining Worldwide MasterMind Groups.

STARSHINE GUIDING PRINCIPLE #15.

World peace is a result of individual peace.
"As long as one unhappy person exists on the earth, we all are in danger."
-Trish McCarty

The first time Terri Mansfield approached me about StarShine being a "Peace School" I was so busily absorbed in making sure that we were complying with all of the laws and paperwork that govern charter schools, I hardly had time to notice anything else. The idea seemed almost foreign to me. Terri was a co-founder of the Arizona Department of Peace Campaign along with Shirley Catanzaro, trying to formulate a way for the United States to re-establish a Department of Peace along with the Department of Defense, to create a more pro-active effort toward building peace in our own neighborhoods, as well as globally. She felt that StarShine was a good example.

At the same time, I have for several years, been good friends with one of the most devoted, caring, capable people I have ever known,

Bill Yotive of the United Nations Global Learning and Teaching Project and Yehoram Ben Shalom, a Peace Ambassador for the U.N. We had all worked on technology projects involving linking students together around the world, as our own focus of contributing toward building peace.

"The StarShine Effect" is what happens when you are immersed in an environment that is full of beauty, support, love, learning and order of whole heart, whole body and whole mind; when you are expected to find happiness and be your best. StarShine is deeply based on the most current research of the brain and mind, but the brain is only a computer that maintains the information that is based on experience and genetics. It is the heart that filters this information to become the mind that talks to us and directs or distracts our actions.

We know that heat and electrical current is emitted from the brain. We have been told that we won't be as cold if we use a cap when we go camping. What many people don't know is that the heart area emits many times this electrical energy. When the heart is hurt, or, worse, closed off because of having been hurt, it will go to many lengths to protect itself from further hurt. In fact, it will cause a person to appear angry and unjustifiably nasty to everyone, sometimes just to avoid further pain. But an open heart, a happy heart, or person, will risk almost anything for a relationship with another living being.

In 2006, Malek Deng walked into my office with our great StarShine Ambassador and Connector, Bob Fishman. Malek, now in his twenties, was from Sudan, Africa. When he was eight years old, in 1987, living in Sudan, he was standing near his uncle when military insurgents of the government began murdering everyone in the streets except for the kids. Malek, terrified, watching his uncle fall to the ground, began to run. He ran and ran, deep into the jungle. By nightfall, there were at least one thousand children running through the jungle with no place to go so they kept running until they collapsed to try to sleep. The children were in grave danger near wild animals, insects and snakes, but they had no choice. They continued to run without knowing where they were going. They watched their friends die along the way. They came upon the Nile River, infested with crocodiles, but knew they had to try to cross. These small children figured out how to make small pods of grass float so they could use the pods to help them to swim. Malek told me of the horror of watching his friends eaten by the lions and crocodiles. But Malek made it to the other side and at times had to eat mud with his friends because they did not know what else to eat.

Malek's story is one of so many *"Lost Boys of Sudan"* who eventually, by the Grace of God, made it to the United States and was able to become educated and eventually a United States citizen.

As Malek told me his story, I could not hold my tears back. How could this person, at one time a small child, have endured so much and still now have a smile on his face? He went on to explain that he had returned to the refugee camp on several occasions to help some of the children still there, mostly orphans from Darfur. He brought supplies to a few kids and helped one of the workers there. The children began to grow in number and asked him to bring them a school. He did establish a school and now had around eight hundred children living in his school near Wau, Sudan and he wanted me to help him.

Bewildered, I looked at Malek's hopeful face as I said, "Malek, this story is incredible. God certainly is working through you. You are blessed beyond almost anything I have heard, but there is no way I can help you. We barely have the money we need to comply with all of the regulations we must adhere to for a school in the United States. And every one of the children in this school has great needs in food, assistance, parenting, and clothes, not to mention education. I don't have any more to give. I wish I could help you but it seems totally impossible for me." Malek looked at me long and hard, and huge tears welled up in his eyes and began to run down his face. He began to cry, "I have no curriculum!" he said, "You must help me!" I had to give in, my heart so heavy, "Okay, Malek, we will figure this out together. I have no idea how I will be helpful, but we will adopt your school. It will be a StarShine Academy and we will figure it out." About two weeks later, the local Rotary chapter elected to give us $1500.00 toward helping Malek and we shipped hundreds of books to the Sudan, StarShine Academy, Our Ladies School.

Malek and I have become very close friends as we have had to face many hurdles together, and I could not be more thankful that we have this work to do with one another. Spending time around Malek and his Sudanese friends, continually reminds me of our similarities as well as our differences. Malek and his friends have had so many hardships, including the trip to the United States and yet they are always laughing, continually giving thanks to God for their blessings. They work so hard on their education and in the work they do, and they all support in some way, their brothers, sisters and loved ones back in Africa. Malek sells tee shirts to earn money for his kids and he works two jobs as well as attends medical school. I don't know when or if he sleeps, but he doesn't complain. Meeting Malek and hearing his stories, including a couple of years ago when the Red Cross found his mother and sisters and brought Malek back for their reunion, makes me ever proud to be an American. When I attended Malek's citizenship ceremony, I watched as so many war-torn refugees became Americans, with intense faces of pride I rarely see as I walk down America's streets.

People, like animals, fight for survival but they continually yearn to learn how to thrive. Peace and happiness, comes from very specific learning and practicing small choices each day. It does not come automatically because our brains are always on the lookout for danger. We are always ready to react, fight or run. But if we are to experience greater personal peace and happiness, we need to know how to accomplish it. We don't know what we don't know and that is what gets us into trouble.

Peace happens when people learn how to decide to be peaceful. If we are terrified, in "fight or flight" we won't be able to allow it to happen. Our brains will tell our bodies to fight with words, thoughts and actions. We will say and do things that make no sense, because our sensible brain shuts down when we are scared or threatened. The only way to be able to overcome these automatic reactions is to develop greater faith, practice more happiness, do balancing poses, even fake laughter and fake smiles, eventually causes more clear thinking. Visualizing your breath moving through your heart, in and out, automatically calms you down. The Beatles sing "Love is all there is" and that is what StarShine teaches.

For several years, StarShine hosted the United Nations Peace Pals Art Contest for children throughout the world. Children submitted artwork depicting their own ideas of "Peace" as each year the theme changed. The words from the Peace Prayer Society, "May Peace Prevail on Earth" were shown on many of the pictures as on our Peace Poles in our gardens. Children from the poorest countries, using primitive paper and crayons sometimes produced the most outstanding pictures.

The reverence for the contest and the art is precious. Unfortunately, the children in the United States submitted some of the least inspired pictures, year after year. We were always surprised as we laid thousands of pictures carefully on the cafeteria floor so we could judge them, everyone always remarked about how glaringly obvious the lack of concern for the art contest was represented in the United States compared to all other countries. It just seemed like the children were motivated to enter the contest but the adults helping them did not obviously inspire the entrants to produce their very best work. It seemed to be an indication of the lack of true commitment and it was prevalent. Just another serious reminder to get our act together now.

We have around thirty thousand pictures from nearly every country, hoping one day to display all of them. An art gallery owner in Phoenix asked to put some of the art in his gallery for a month-long show a few years ago. He wanted to record reactions of his patrons when they walked into the gallery, lined floor to ceiling with children's Peace Art, showing only the pictures without any explanation. Adults would walk into the gallery, curious from seeing the pictures through the front glass window; they would stop and begin to stare at the pictures and inevitably begin to cry. The messages found deep inside of these drawings, interpreted by children from around the world, explained the same thing. They all understood and were able to portray what peace looks like. Children, like animals, can be our greatest teachers if only we begin to quiet ourselves, observe and absorb what they say. They all want peace; they know what it looks like, but they look to adults to show them the way. If we are going to have babies, we all have a responsibility to raise them up in the most admirable way. Each one of us, even those without children can help to inspire the ones around us to be their best. If you have extra finances, please help a school, but even if you don't have extra money or extra time to volunteer, help others with a genuine smile or an encouraging word or even a pat on the back. You could change someone's life in a small gesture.

13

THE END OF THE BEGINNING: A WHOLE NEW WORLD ...THE NEXT CHAPTER

"Nihil nisi optimo". "nothing but the best"
Roman orator, Cicero

An old Chinese saying goes something like this: If I only have a (dime) left to spend, let me spend one nickel on bread and the other on a flower. For one feeds the body, but the other, more important, feeds the soul.

"Ladies and gentlemen, this is your captain. I have some bad news." This is not what I wanted to hear. Steve and I had just left the Big Island of Hawaii, after Steve had played in a concert the night before in a reunion with the Steve Miller Band. We were headed for home and we were in a big rain and thunderstorm, flying in the middle of a big cloud and it was dark outside. "We just lost our navigation and radar system. They are trying to keep the other planes away from us. We are going to try to land in Maui." Ughhh! People around me started crying and one lady kept saying "Oh God" until I asked her to stop. My stomach was in knots like everyone else and I was wishing the pilot had not shared this news with us. I, like probably everyone else on that flight, started praying really hard that we would be safe. I kept saying over and over, a prayer I learned years ago:

The light of God surrounds me
The love of God enfolds me
Wherever I am; God is and
All is well.
I am the light that God shines through
For He and I are One; not two
He wants me where and as, I Am

So I'll not fear, nor will, nor plan
For if I Am relaxed and free
Then He'll work out His plan
Through me.

It was December 11 and I was already anxious and needed to get home to move our entire school to a new location during StarShine's Christmas break. So when the plane's turbulence became progressively worse than any I had ever experienced, I was terrified. So many thoughts were racing in my head, of course about my family but also many about our schools and children. It always seems like everything goes into slow motion when life is completely out of control and this was a perfect example. There were a few moments of total peace that washed over me, with a couple of thoughts of total release to "everything is perfect and the way it is supposed to be." I can't explain how I went back and forth from terror to peace in my mind and body, but I did.

And, you figured, we bumpily landed but safely, due to our great pilots. And after several hours on the ground, waiting for our plane to be repaired, they cancelled our flight and transported us to a nearby hotel.

But it wasn't just any hotel. It was the Makena Beach and Golf Resort, one of the most beautiful hotels in Maui, Hawaii. I was exhausted from being awake all night, having experienced the hair-raising trouble with our flight and the stormy weather. But as I stood on our balcony, overlooking the peaceful ocean, while watching the sun rise, I felt an overwhelming understanding about StarShine and faith.

Less than twelve hours before, I didn't know if I would ever see another day, but I chose *not* to lose faith. And now I was looking at Paradise surrounded by a calm sea. It seemed like a metaphor for life and for StarShine. It was the silver lining around a black cloud or the darkest night before the dawn. This was yet another example of my mom's words coming back to remind me that everything always works out the way it is supposed to. We keep taking one more step in faith, always without knowing exactly where we will end up.

Less than thirty days before, I did not know where or how I would be able to move our original school to a new location. After nearly a year of knowing that we were supposed to arrange for a place to relocate, our landlord, the Arizona Episcopal Diocese, had given us an ultimatum to be out. We had to move from our school site by December 15th and we did not have certainty about where we were going to move. We had been negotiating to purchase the new school site for about eight months but it wasn't coming together. Problems with everything including investors, closing and financing kept delaying our ability to move and now, at the beginning of December, we still did not have the property in our possession.

As I looked at this picture-perfect ocean view, everything seemed perfect, but it wasn't. This week was the last week of school before the break and we had to make moving arrangements, without a place to go. I called Jan and told her that no matter what, even with me being away, we had to get the move going and I would continually work on trying to get the new property to close.

Jan, Rich Rose our CFO, and Tom Woodward, our Director of Strategic Partnerships, back at the school, decided to start to move everything out of the classrooms into large semi-trailers in case we had to store everything for a while. They could not find any workers because all of the moving companies we could possibly afford were already booked for Christmas and Holiday moves. So Tom and Rich went down to the homeless shelter, in downtown Phoenix, to find some workers. What they found were eight angels.

They found men so excited about having work for Christmas that they worked harder than any movers you have ever seen. The sadder part of this story is that three of the men were veterans. It still completely bothers me that in a country like America, we can treat veterans the way we do. They give their lives to serve American people and we allow them to become homeless. We are so ready to throw away real people in this country, misfit children, elderly, mentally challenged, physically challenged, people who wear different clothes or have different hair and veterans. When will we learn?

So they figured out how to get the kids and teachers to learn and teach how moving happens and to get everything out by December 15th, our drop-dead date when they told us they would change the locks on the property. This still presented a problem as there were two school days before school was out for the holiday and we needed to continue school. StarShine staff got together and decided that the teachers could take the kids to the science museums and use the field trips as classrooms.

This is StarShine. Nobody wastes time blaming or complaining. No shame, blame or victim here. They look at what is going on and make decisions to do the best they can. StarShine people empower their choices, even when the choices seem bleak.

In the mean time, as I was negotiating my way back home from Hawaii, I was glued to my phone, trying to work on what I hoped would be final terms for the property we wanted on McDowell Road so that it could close. StarShine Academy's flagship needed a home right now!

We flew all night on Tuesday and went straight to the school Wednesday morning to check on how things were going. It was now December 14th and still a ton of stuff to move. Driving up to the property, seeing the three huge semi trucks along with a few U-Hauls made my stomach sink. Was this the sweet place I had been for the past ten years of such hard work, now looking like several tornadoes just passed through? I was so tired, everything just seemed like too much to understand for my fried brain.

On top of everything going on at the school, I had previously scheduled our usual year-end Board meeting for December 16th which was two days away, and could hardly bare facing the board with the news that we were moving without having closed on the other property.

Another angel was in the wings though, Senator Mike Morley from Utah. A month or so earlier, he had heard about our problems with buying the new property and had come down to Arizona to see if he could help me. His company, M-13 Construction, Inc. and his financial partners, Entertainment Properties Trust, really liked StarShine's concept to change K-12 education and had been involved in building several charter schools and other buildings throughout the country. They know what is working and what is not working in K-12 and they, like me, care deeply about our country's future. They believed in me and in StarShine. Both of them had doubts about whether they would be able to process paperwork fast enough and overcome a bunch of property problems so that the school could move as quickly as we needed to.

As Mike and I feverously traded phone call and email messages every day, we eliminated problems one by one that included engineering problems, gas leaks, asbestos problems, fire marshal requirements, seller demands and city ordinances. And his financial partners worked as rapidly as possible to get the legal and lending papers together and finalized. Since Mike was in town, I invited him to come to our board meeting on Friday.

When Friday morning arrived, I was very thankful. The school was really now a "School in a Box" having been completely moved out of the old property and into semi-trailers. Mike had performed so many miracles along with everyone else, it looked as if the closing would occur on Friday afternoon. StarShine's Board met at our favorite breakfast spot, the Airport Marriot Hotel, to talk about StarShine's past and our future. Each person spoke for a few minutes about what StarShine meant to them.

Shep Gordon talked about why he was only on two boards; one for StarShine and one for the Dalai Lama. With tears in his eyes and mine, he described how much his children meant to him and how every time he sent them to school they were bullied or made fun of. In his gentle, quiet way of speaking, he urged everyone to help StarShine so that all kids could learn to be more than anything we have ever seen before.

And then Mike received a phone call. He motioned to me that he needed to talk to me. He said that we couldn't close; there was a cloud on the property preventing the title company from being able to give us a clear title. He explained that a neighbor had been using the property for several years to drive to the back of his house, but no access had ever been legally conveyed, so it created a legal access problem. He said not only was it a nearly impossible problem, it could possibly take months or years to resolve it. I couldn't believe it, or I wouldn't. I said that I would go talk to the neighbor to see if he would be willing to sign an agreement. Mike suggested that it might not be a good idea, but I would not agree. I said, I have kids to move and I will figure this out. In the mean time, Mike had called an engineer to meet him at the property to try to determine a fair way to deal with this problem, so he left the breakfast.

Nearly in shock, I sat down, trying to appear better than numb. And Vernon stood up to describe his relationship with StarShine and to introduce his daughter, Caroline. She had been invited by me because she is working on designing what the future of a classroom might look like, as she interns with StarShine and her college.

Vernon Swaback, as eloquent as ever, told his story about Frank Lloyd Wright's dream of community. He spoke of his own quest to rebuild communities where less is more and where beauty and function are the priority for design and architecture, rather than more square feet. He talked about his hope for the new property and how it might become a beam of possibilities for communities throughout the world, representing not only a new way to learn but a new way to live together in peace, camaraderie and beauty. My heart was sinking.

I told everyone about the problem with the property and that I needed to go over to see if perhaps I could reason with the neighbor fast enough to solve all of our issues. So I left before the breakfast and board meeting ended.

When Steve and I arrived at the property, Mike and the engineer were talking with the neighbors and it looked like they were taking measurements on the ground. I introduced myself and my husband

Steve, and started to talk to the main neighbor as well as some other neighbors who had walked up. They were all very nice, but I could tell they had some issues with trusting what we were saying and how fast things needed to be resolved. I kept quietly praying about all of this, but my stomach was flipping, knowing I had all of the semi-trucks with no place to go, full of school equipment.

Just then, Jan drove up and got out of the car, smiling and saying hello to everyone. As she was talking to the main neighbor, she stopped, looked inquisitively toward him and said, "I think we graduated together." Sure enough, he actually had their yearbook in his house, so he turned around to run in to get it and ran right back out with the page opened to Jan's face!!

Now, even for StarShine stories, this one will go down in history! The entire tone of conversation changed. Mike called his lawyer to draw up a legal description protecting both the neighbor's access and our property. The neighbors all signed the agreements and we closed the property by 4:00 on that Friday, about ten minutes before our semi-trucks arrived to begin to unload!

This story could have made a book all alone, as the upheavals of moving the school or not began several years prior to this. But wanting to stick to the main reason I wrote this book was to try to give you some hope for the future; that there are answers and there are people you can trust to give the right answers so we all don't have to learn the hard way.

Magic happens when people agree to do anything; positive or negative. The Bible explains it, "Where two or more are gathered...nothing is impossible." StarShine has proven it over and over again and we are teaching it to the children, teachers, parents and community.

Miracle on 35th Street

So it was the week before Christmas and we had our property with some money borrowed, to build some new buildings and fix up the old ones. And we had homeless people working thirteen hours a day for cash at the end of each evening. And we had teachers choosing to fix up their classrooms rather than take a holiday. And we had the neighbors helping us with everything we were doing, while Dory delivered small poinsettias throughout the neighborhood businesses, just to introduce ourselves.

Tom worked thirteen-hour days and drove our workers back and forth, totally devoted to helping them. Minko, one of our CPAs, and Tom's favorite companion, used his world-class rock climbing abilities to climb on everything to fix it. Lynne Ericksson emptied boxes and ran all over town buying used furniture. She completely set up my office, and the rest of the administration area, while taking photos of everything to continue to document our history.

By January 2, 2012, we were mostly ready for the kids to come back so we could start their second annual StarShine Student Boot Camp. They were so excited, they didn't even complain about a new, more rigid dress code, in fact they seemed to be more proud than ever.

By the end of the first week of January, Vernon Swaback and his associates, Jeff Denzak and Pau Figue had the beginnings of the Master Plan completed for our "Creative Community and Learning Center Eco-Village" K-12+ community and we had scheduled a meeting for our building permits for the following week with the City of Phoenix.

Tom had already made contact with the different branches of the military to help us with our planned "Military Obstacle Course: Overcoming Obstacles," so we could give constant appreciation to those men and women who serve our country. We will use Tom's favorite quote on the course: *"Life is an obstacle course. I am the chief obstacle."*

We are working on big ideas for our Global Connections Innovation and Technology Center, crafted after the NASA Space Command Center so the kids can have constant contact with our schools throughout the world, while being immersed in high-tech science. And the Elder's Wisdom Center will be my favorite...maybe because I want to prepare a place for myself someday. But also to give respect and tribute to the shoulders we all stand upon; to keep our history and our individual customs, cultures and celebrations in the front and center of what new knowledge we might learn each day.

This little StarShine Eco-community has reached into the hearts and souls of so many. Not just the kids we have saved and not just their parents, but StarShine has deeply touched the most amazing dignitaries and scientists of our world today, as it has me. And I know the world will be different because of it. Too many people have witnessed the potential of hope and change that exists today, not to also help to bring about a total transformation of how we view life and one another. Not only do we need a complete overhaul of our K-12 education system, but a complete overhaul of the way we choose to live; how we make choices and how we begin to honor our own existence.

I look forward to living in the world that values souls, love and beauty more than stuff, and spending time talking and truly listening with others at least as much as texting. And while I wait for the rest of the world to find it, I will enjoy walking through ours; this small but magical village of learning, sharing, experiencing and growing; an almost perfect place on earth; StarShine.

And what's next? What is the new vision? It is a continuation of the same vision we started with, "To change education for every single child on the planet, so each can find what each one needs to realize their own dreams and to make society better." We have created a data network to efficiently link schools together to share best ideas and best practices and to continually improve, while doing the best at any given time. We see schools sharing resources and buying power to lower costs. We see green technology and beautiful schools that don't look like prisons anymore. We see creative community schools, independently operated by and for the unique community they are in. We see kids learning how to garden and eat, exercise and enjoy nature to be healthy. We see children learning about the things that really matter in life and that they aren't things. We see kids excited about how smart they are becoming. We see education being the honorable thing it should be and teachers being among the most famous and highly paid leaders, of our citizens. We see StarShine replacing the word "school" as in, "I have to go do a little "StarShine" before I go out."

There exists vast support mechanisms today that did not exist when we first started. Our dream is to grow 11,000 independent, small, accredited uniquely owned and operated community-based schools together within the next five years: to leverage, not rule one another, but to share common goals, intelligence, amazing people and to make the world better, while supporting individual dreamers.

Each day at StarShine, we do our best to love the kids and give them information that eventually leads them to wisdom to inspire them to continually seek and grow their own knowledge.

Yesterday, I met a most unusual young man, an eight year old teacher named Chief of the Clouds, in his Hopi name. He had great wisdom to explain to me about taking care of one another, especially our family. He shared with me the things he wants schools to teach, especially the things, most important. He is attending a school that is teaching him how to speak his native Hopi language and he is very proud of his roots and his family. He sang for me, he danced for me and he recited his native Hopi language, so beautiful. His mother, a most unusual single mother, also imparted wisdom to me. She said, "We don't think we are spiritual or more caring or more understanding. We are just Hopi, this is our way. We are brought up to be this way. This is our way."

As much as StarShine has taught to me, I marvel at how much I need to continue to learn.

APPENDIX

www.trishmccarty.com
www.thestarshineeffect.com
www.starshineacademy.org

Find links to joining worldwide mastermind groups.
Excellent free download forms:
ABC *Get Organized and Stop Forgetting Things*

Bassoff, Michael 2001 "Relation Shift: Revolutionary Fundraising"
www.rdpublishers.com

Bidgoli, Hossein 2004 "The Internet Encyclopedia Volume 1"
http://www.wiley.com/WileyCDA/

Cameron, Julia 1992 "The Artist's Way" http://us.penguingroup.com

Canfield, Jack 2005 "Success Principles"
http://www.harpercollins.com

Clinebell Ph.D., Howard 1996 "Ecotherapy: Healing Ourselves Healing
the Earth" http://www.augsburgfortress.org/

Coelho, Paulo 1995 "The Alchemist" http://www.harpercollins.com

Elliot, Jay 2011 "The Steve Jobs way: iLeadership for a New
Generation" www.perseusbooks.com www.vanguardpressbooks.com

Evans, Henry J. 2012 "The Hour A Day Entrepreneur"
www.HoursADayBook.com

Friedman, Thomas L. 2011 "That Used to Be Us" www.fsgbooks.com

Haanel, Charles F. 2007 "The Master Key System"
www.ArcManor.com

Hess, Frederick M. 2010 "The Same Thing Over and Over" www.hup.harvard.edu

Heuston, Dustin Hull 2011 "The Third Source" www.waterford.org

INC Magazine

Millman, Dan 2012 "Science of Mind" www.devorss.com

Pink, Daniel H. 2009 "Drive: The Surprising Truth About What Motivates Us" www.danpink.com

Redfield, James 1997 "The Celestine Prophecy" Warner Books http://www.hachettebookgroup.com

Slayter, Jeff 2011 "Champions Knockout Strategies" www.celebritypresspublishing.com

Stewart, Vivien 2012 "A World- Class Education" www.ascd.org/books

Pearl, Dr. Eric 2001 "The Reconnection: Heal Others, Heal Yourself" www.hayhouse.com

University of Pennsylvania http://www.ppc.sas.upenn.edu/moreteachingresources.htm

ABOUT THE AUTHOR

Patricia A. McCarty (Trish A.), is the Founder and CEO of Education Resources, StarShine Academy International Schools and StarShine Planet. Considered one of the leading innovators in K-12 education reform, she began life with a world view, as an Air Force dependent and was born in Frankfurt, Germany and spent time growing up in Tokyo, Japan. With a deep interest in health, neuroscience and well being, she went to college in Durango, Colorado, hoping to become a medical technologist with a focus on making people ultimately healthy. She became disappointed in the medical field due to its focus on disease and medicine, rather than health. It was then that Trish began a lifelong interest in studying fitness, well-being and healthy brain function.

She was recruited from college to be fast-tracked as a young female executive for AT&T in bringing women into the industry in leadership positions and she worked as an executive for Mellon Bank and later, founded a bank. It was here that Trish formed her beginning ideas of what should be taught in school to bring about academic and life success, starting in kindergarten. She has founded several companies, has won numerous honors and is frequently quoted in the media and as a featured speaker.

Steve McParter
6005 E. LINCOLN DR.
Paradise Valley, AZ

85253

(H.) 480-998-5851
(c.) 480-220-1132

steve@stevemccarty.net

Made in the USA
Charleston, SC
11 December 2012

16255331R00150